CODING UNLOCKED
UNLOCKED
SCRATCH AND PYTHON: the basics

USEFUL INFORMATION

SCRATCH

Scratch website: http://scratch.mit.edu

Username:

Password:

PYTHON

Python website: www.scholastic.co.uk/python

HYWEL CARVER

script · loop · variable · print("coding")

CODING UNLOCKED
SCRATCH AND PYTHON: the basics

repeat · string · if else

SCHOLASTIC

Scholastic Children's Books
Euston House, 24 Eversholt Street,
London NW1 1DB, UK

A division of Scholastic Ltd
London ~ New York ~ Toronto ~ Sydney ~ Auckland
Mexico City ~ New Delhi ~ Hong Kong

First published in the UK by Scholastic Ltd, 2015

Text by Hywel Carver
Illustrations by Simon Letchford
© Scholastic Children's Books, 2015

ISBN 978 1407 15941 6

Printed in China

2 4 6 8 10 9 7 5 3 1

Papers used by Scholastic Children's Books are
made from wood grown in sustainable forests.

Scratch is developed by the Lifelong Kindergarten Group at the MIT Media Lab.
See http://scratch.mit.edu

CONTENTS

INTRODUCTION

This is a book all about learning to code. Coding is probably the most useful thing you can ever learn to do because it's how you can make machines do what you want them to do. Coding will let you make fun games and cool websites. It'll let you control robots and build clever machines. Coding is involved in everything from electronic toys to life-saving medical equipment, and from mobile phones to rocket ships. So let's get started!

Here's the first big important secret about coding that you really need to know. Ready? Computers, tablets and phones are actually very, very stupid. They only ever do things people tell them to do. It's true that computers can do things that we can't, and sometimes they can seem to be very clever, but that's only because a coder has told them what to do.

 A coder just means someone who writes code.

Because computers are very stupid, they will do exactly what you tell them without really understanding what you mean. That's the second big (and important) secret about coding: computers do exactly what you tell them, nothing more and nothing less. That means that you have to be very careful and precise when telling a computer what to do.

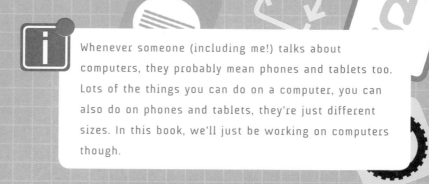

Whenever someone (including me!) talks about computers, they probably mean phones and tablets too. Lots of the things you can do on a computer, you can also do on phones and tablets, they're just different sizes. In this book, we'll just be working on computers though.

If we were sitting at a table eating breakfast, and I said, "Please pass the nilk", you would probably guess that I had meant to say "milk" not "nilk" without even thinking about it. But a computer wouldn't. To a computer, "milk" and "Milk" can be totally different things, because one has a capital letter and the other doesn't. " milk" and "milk" aren't the same thing to a computer because one has a space at the beginning and the other doesn't. So be as careful as possible with what you tell a computer to do, because they're very stupid and they might not understand you.

Code is like a recipe – it tells the computer what you want it to do, and how it should do it. Computers read code from the top of the page downwards, doing each step in turn. And just like a recipe shows you how to create food, your code will make a program.

A recipe for computers is normally called an **algorithm**. An algorithm is a series of steps that tells the computer what you want it to do. Let's try an example – an algorithm for brushing your teeth. We need to break it down into simple steps that even a computer could follow.

1. Pick up the toothpaste in one hand
2. Open the lid of the toothpaste
3. Pick up the toothbrush in your other hand
4. Hold the toothbrush so that the bristles are under the open end of the toothpaste
5. Gently squeeze a small amount of toothpaste onto the toothbrush bristles
6. Close the toothpaste lid
7. Put down the toothpaste
8. Turn on the tap with your free hand
9. Hold the toothbrush so that the bristles are under the running water for 5 seconds
10. Turn off the tap with your free hand
11. Hold the toothbrush so that the bristles are pressing against your teeth
12. Move the toothbrush in small circles so that the bristles move against your teeth and gums
13. Go back to step 12 until you have brushed all of your teeth
14. Spit out the toothpaste
15. Turn on the tap with your free hand
16. Rinse the toothbrush under the running water
17. Wash out your mouth with water
18. Turn off the tap
19. Put down the toothbrush

Brushing your teeth looks so complicated when you write it down, but each step is something you do completely naturally when you brush your teeth every day. Writing algorithms is all about breaking something down into these precise but simple instructions, so that you can tell a computer how to do it.

Now it's your turn! Try writing down your own algorithms (step-by-step instructions) for:
- Making toast
- Playing the card game, Snap
- Your journey to school

Remember to include every single step to create clear and detailed instructions. Imagine you're teaching a robot how to do each task!

The more you see code, the more you'll be able to read it like a recipe. It might look a bit confusing to start with, but as you read and write more code it'll soon start to look more familiar.

Writing code is the part where we decide exactly what steps the algorithm should do, but that doesn't mean the computer will go ahead and do those steps straight away. That's all done in a second part, where we **run** the code. One of the brilliant things about code is that once you've written it, it's easy to run it as many times as you like.

In the same way that a recipe could be written in English, French, German or Spanish, computer code can be written in lots of different languages too. But they're all just different ways of saying the same thing.

In this book, things that are in code will be shown in a special format like this:

```
this would be a piece of code.
```

Here are some different ways of saying "Hello coder!" in a variety of different computer languages.

Scratch:

Python 3: `print("Hello coder!")`

Java: `System.out.println("Hello coder!");`

Ruby: `puts "Hello coder!"`

JavaScript: `alert("Hello coder!");`

You can see that they all use different words and punctuation to tell the computer what to do. Each language tells the computer what to do in a different way, which is why you have to be careful with what you type. Remember the two secret rules of coding: computers are very stupid, and they'll try to do exactly what you tell them to. The same word or symbol might mean something different in different languages, so it might not have the effect you intended.

ABOUT THIS BOOK

In this book, we're going to learn two different programming languages. The first one is called Scratch, which you might already know from school. Scratch is a language designed to help people learn to code, and you can use it to make animations, games and lots of other cool stuff.

The second language we're going to learn is called Python. Python is used all over the world for all kinds of things. Professional coders use it to make search engines like Google, chart-topping games, cool websites and amazing animations.

In each chapter you'll learn something new about coding, then see how to do it in both Scratch and Python. There'll be a little puzzle adventure to solve with Python, and a project to make in Scratch, so you can show off what you've learned.

Why not spend some time at the end of each chapter playing with the skills you've learned before moving on to the next one? Try changing the code or adding to it, using what you've learned, to create something that no one else in the world has ever made. This book will give you a basic understanding of how to code, and give you some fun, simple projects to work on. But, like any new skill, the more you explore and practise, the more you'll learn. Soon you'll be a coding expert!

SCRATCH AND PYTHON

Let's quickly compare the two coding languages you're going to learn in this book, before we look at each one in more detail.

Scratch works with colourful blocks that you can drag and drop together to make code. It's useful for making fun games and cool animations. Each block tells Scratch to do a single thing, and they can be joined together to make chunks of code, called scripts. Scratch is a great coding language for learning, but there are some things that it can't do, which require a more advanced programming language.

Python can be used for almost every kind of coding, and is used by many professional coders around the world. You can use Python to create your own custom version of Minecraft, to create complex websites and to code for Raspberry Pi computers. It's also used by big computing companies like Google and Microsoft. You can do more advanced programming with Python than Scratch so it's more complex, but it's still easy to read and write. Python code is written by typing text, rather than dragging and dropping blocks.

In this book, you don't have to choose between Python and Scratch. We're going to look at them both together to understand the most important concepts of coding – in both languages – so that you really understand how to write code.

GETTING STARTED WITH SCRATCH

To start using Scratch, open a web browser on your computer and go to http://scratch.mit.edu, which is the address of the Scratch homepage. From here you can see some examples of Scratch projects made by other people, but we're going to dive straight into making our own projects.

Scratch will work on any computer that runs Flash. That means it should work on most Mac, Windows and Linux computers, but not tablets or phones.

If you already have a Scratch account from school you can skip the first step.

Creating a Scratch account

First of all, ask an adult to help you create an account on the Scratch website. You don't need to create an account, but having an account will let you save everything you make with Scratch so that you can always find it again, and it's totally free. To create an account, click on the Join Scratch button in the top-right corner, then fill out the boxes that appear with a username and a password that you'll remember. You'll need to enter the same password twice to move onto the next step. Write your username and password at the front of this book (see page 2) so you don't forget them.

Make sure your username doesn't match your real name, and remember to choose a password that no one else will be able to guess. This is really important for staying safe online.

Once you've done that, Scratch will ask you which month and year you were born in, what your gender is and which country you're from. It'll also ask for an email address, so they can help you reset your password in case you ever forget it. Make sure you ask for your parents' permission before using their email address. Scratch doesn't give this information out to anyone else, or display it anywhere on the website.

Now you've created an account, click the "OK Let's Go!" button, and you'll be logged in. If you're logged in, you should be able to see the username you chose in the top-right corner of the page.

If you come back to Scratch and you want to sign in, click on the "Sign in" button in the top-right corner, and enter the username and password you used when you created your Scratch account.

The project screen

To start a new Scratch project, click on the Create button from the menu at the top and you'll be taken to the project editor.

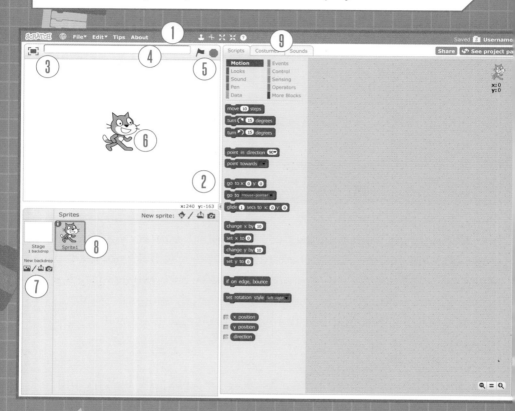

This screen is where we'll create all of our Scratch projects, so let's get to know it a bit.

At the top, there's a menu bar (1),which contains options for creating a new project (under the File menu), and for deleting and duplicating things with the rubber stamp and scissors icons. It also has the menu for your Scratch username, which lets you see your profile, and all of the projects you've made (by clicking on My Stuff).

The box in the top-left of the screen is called the stage area (2). The stage is the Scratch word for the area where we see what our Scratch project is doing. It's where you can play the games you build, and see the animations you create. At the top of the stage you can see a button to make the stage full-screen (3), which you can always reverse by pressing the matching button once the stage is full-screen. There's also a box where you can give a name to your project (4) the green flag button (which is the button to start your project running once you've built it) and the red stop button which you can use to stop your projects running (5).

Every new project starts by showing the Scratch cat sprite (6) (sometimes called Scratch Junior, or Scratch Jr.) in the stage. Sprites are the characters and objects in your projects that do things like talking, moving, asking questions and making sounds.

Underneath the stage, you'll see a picture of the stage background (a plain white rectangle at the moment) and the sprite list. Underneath the stage picture are options for creating new backdrops (7), which are new backgrounds for your project. Backdrops are the pictures that stay still behind your sprites, to set the scenery of your animations or show where your games are taking place. You can't do all the same things with backdrops as you can with sprites, but they're really helpful for creating and displaying scenery that isn't going to change very much.

In the column on the left there are options to create new backdrops by choosing from existing Scratch backdrops, or by drawing your own. At this point, there's only one backdrop, the plain white one.

The larger panel shows all of the sprites in your Scratch project (8). At the moment, that's just the Scratch cat, but there are options for making extra sprites by choosing from a pre-made sprite in the Scratch library, or by drawing your own.

Try clicking on the picture of the stage background under the stage itself, so that a light blue box appears around it, and the right-hand side of the screen will give you options for coding the stage. There are tabs at the top for creating Scripts, Backdrops and Sounds (9). Scripts are how you add animation, sounds and lots of other exciting things to your project. The Backdrops tab shows a list of all the backgrounds you've created for your project, and lets you create new ones. The Sounds tab shows all the sounds you have created, and lets you create more.

If you now click on the picture of the Scratch cat in the sprite list, so that the light-blue rectangle appears around it, the right-hand side will change again so that you have options for coding the cat. These include Scripts and Sounds (just like when you clicked on the picture of the stage) but also includes an option for Costumes. This is where you can create different appearances for your sprites. Select the Scratch cat in the bottom left, then click on the Costumes tab on the right side of the screen. You'll see two costumes for this sprite. If you click between the two costumes as fast as you can, it'll look like the cat is dancing!

Scripts and blocks

With the Scratch cat selected in the bottom left, click on the Scripts tab. This is where you'll be doing most of the coding for your projects, so we should get to know it now.

A script is an algorithm made up of blocks. Blocks are individual instructions to Scratch that might tell it to move one of our sprites, change the costume of the Scratch cat, or play a sound.

The central column of your screen is the block palette. This contains all of the different blocks you can use to construct your scripts. All the blocks are grouped and colour-coded into different categories, which are the options shown at the top of the palette.

We're going to start with only a few of them:
- Motion lets you move and turn your sprites.
- Looks lets you make your sprites say things, get larger or change costumes.
- Sound lets you make your sprites make sounds or play musical notes.
- Events lets you write code that runs when a button is clicked or a keyboard key is pressed.

You'll learn much more about different types of blocks later in this book.

To the right of the block palette is the script area. This is where you can drag and drop blocks to create the scripts that control your program.

A Scratch program

Let's make our first program with Scratch! First of all, make sure you're in a new project with no changes. Make sure you've got the Scratch cat selected in the sprite list, and you're on the Scripts tab on the right-hand side.

1. Click on Events in the block palette, choose the "when green flag clicked" block, and drag and drop it into the middle of the scripts area.

2. Now, click on Motion in the block palette, and find the "move 10 steps" block. Drag it into the scripts area, and hold it underneath the "when green flag clicked" block. Before you drop it, you should see a thin white line appear underneath the top block. That's Scratch telling you that this block will fit underneath the top one. Now drop the "move 10 steps" block and you'll see that they fit together snugly.

3. The 10 in the "move 10 steps" block has a white background. That tells you that it can be changed. Let's change it to 5 by clicking on the 10, deleting it, and typing 5 instead.

4. Next, let's use the "say Hello! for 2 secs" block. It's inside the Looks block palette. Drag it underneath the "move 5 steps" block until you see the white line, then drop it so they lock together.

5. Okay, it's time to see what we've made so far! Click on any of the blocks in your script to preview what the script does. You should see the cat move to the right on the stage, and a speech bubble will appear over its head saying "Hello!". Cool!

You can always preview your scripts by clicking on them. Try previewing it again, but this time watch the script itself. You'll see a faint yellow glow around it – that helps you know that your script is running. The glow will disappear when the script stops.

Scripts in Scratch run down the page. Scratch will start at the top block, then run the block underneath it, and the block underneath that until it gets to the bottom of the script. Scratch blocks have a little bump on their bottom-left corner which fits into the little gap on the top-left corner of other blocks, so you know that they go together. Event blocks don't have the little gap on the top left because they are always the first block in a script, which makes sure you can't go wrong with them. Some of the blocks are different shapes, so you know they fit in different places. We'll learn more about them later.

6. Let's add one more block to this script, so that our cat makes some noise. Click on the Sound palette, find the "play sound meow" block, and drag it to go between the "move 5 steps" and "say Hello! for 2 secs" blocks. This time the white line will appear between the two blocks. When you drop the block, it will go in between them.

When you try to move a block that's already in a script, Scratch will also move any blocks joined underneath it but not blocks joined above. So if you want to move a whole script, you need to drag the top block in the script, but if you want to remove a block that's in the middle of a script, you have to do it in two steps:
1. move the block out with all of the blocks beneath it
2. move back all the blocks you moved out except for the top one.

You already know that you can preview your script by clicking on it, but this script begins with the event "when green flag clicked". So try running the script by clicking on the green flag at the top right of the stage. You should see the cat move, say "Hello!" and you'll hear your computer make a meow sound!

GETTING STARTED WITH PYTHON

Normally with Python, you'd have to download and install a program onto your computer to run Python programs. However, all the Python you need in this book can be done online, for free! All you need to do is go to www.scholastic.co.uk/python and you can run all your Python code there. This will work on Mac, Windows and Linux computers, most tablet computers and most smartphones too.

Go to www.scholastic.co.uk/python now and you should see a box with a black background. This is called a **terminal**, where we type code into Python and see the results. The screen will be plain black to start with, but as soon as Python is ready and listening to you, you'll see

followed by a flashing line. This is called a **prompt** – it tells you that Python is listening to what you tell it to do.

Python is a text-based language, which means we have to type in whatever we want it to do. It also means we have to be very careful with what we type. If you make a mistake when typing something, Python won't know what you meant to do. Remember, computers are very stupid!

Now let's try our first program! After the prompt, type:

```
>>> print("Hello Python coder!")
```

and then press Enter or Return. Pressing Return tells Python that you've finished typing, and that it should run your code.

As soon as you press Enter, you should see this:

```
>>> print("Hello Python coder!")
Hello Python coder!
>>>
```

You've just run your first Python program! Now let's understand what we did. The first line is what you typed in. The word **print** is a command, which tells Python to write something. The words it writes will be everything inside the brackets (and). Telling Python to print isn't the same as printing something out onto a piece of paper — it just means writing text onto the terminal so that you can see it. The brackets work like capital letters and full stops. Just like a sentence starts with a capital letter and ends with a full stop, the thing we want Python to print should be inside a left bracket and a right bracket.

In this case we want Python to print the phrase **Hello Python coder!**. Whenever you want to use one or more words in Python, you have to put them inside speech marks, so that Python knows to treat them as words, rather than more commands (like print). Again, like sentences that begin with a capital letter and end with a full stop, words and phrases in Python begin with a " and end with a ". Don't worry too much about this yet! We're just getting the hang of how Python looks and works. You'll learn more about this in the next chapter.

The second line is Python doing exactly what you told it to: saying **Hello Python coder!**. This is the only line that doesn't start with a

>>>

because prompts are only shown when Python is listening to us, not when Python is talking to us.

The third line is a new prompt – Python has done what you told it to, and is ready for your next command!

Let's try a few more uses of print in Python. Try typing in each of these, then pressing Enter.

```
>>> print("Coding in Python is fun!")
>>> print("Computers only do what you tell them to")
>>> print(123456789)
```

Did you notice what was different in the last line? We didn't need to put in any speech marks. That's because what we're telling Python to print is a number, not a word or sentence, and numbers don't need to start and finish with a " like words and sentences do. Again, don't worry too much about this yet – we'll get into more detail in the next chapter.

Errors

When Python doesn't understand what we're trying to do, it'll produce an error message to try to help. These aren't as scary as they seem: errors only happen because computers are stupid. Python errors will try to tell you what type of misunderstanding happened, which can be helpful in fixing bugs.

A bug is a mistake in computer code that means it doesn't do what you intended. But why are they called bugs? The first computers were huge machines made of metal wires, large tubes and magnetic tape, and could easily take up a whole room. In 1947, a computer scientist was trying to work out why their computer wasn't working, and eventually worked out it was because a moth had flown onto one of the circuit boards of the computer! There really was a bug in the system! The name stuck, and we use the word 'bug' these days to mean any problem with computer code. Similarly, the word 'debugging' means finding problems (or bugs) in your code, and fixing the problems.

Let's write some code with an error and see what happens. Try typing in the following code and pressing Enter. We wanted to tell Python to say the word code, but we forgot to put it in speech marks.

```
>>> print(code)
```

Python should immediately tell you that there's been a problem, by saying something that begins with `Traceback` and ends with `NameError: code`

The first lines are trying to show you where in your code the error happened. Because we've only typed one line of code, we don't need help working out where the error happened, but the last line is Python telling you that it doesn't understand what you mean with the word code. It can't tell you exactly how to fix the error, but it does try to point you in the right direction.

Here are some common problems with Python code, and how to fix them. Look at this chart if you ever need help debugging your code.

Spelling Mistakes	Make sure you've copied the code correctly, and check all your spellings.
Using the wrong quotes	Make sure you've used " instead of '.
Missing speech marks	Make sure you use " at the start and end of strings of words.
Mixing upper case and lower case	Make sure you've used the right one each time. Python commands like `print` should always be lower case.
Mixing minus – and underscore _	It's easy to confuse these, so make sure you've used the right one each time.
Using the wrong brackets	Most computers have 3 types of brackets: ( ) [ ] { }. In Python, you'll almost always want the first type: (and). Make sure you remember to use brackets when you print something too.
Using the wrong indentation	Indentation means extra spaces at the beginning of a line – Python will produce errors if there are too many (or not enough) spaces.

Python version	This book uses Python 3, so make sure you're using that, not Python 2 – you can see which version you're using when you start using Python. If the version number begins with a 3 (e.g. 3.0.1), you're using the right version.
Anything else	Ask someone else to check through your code using this list.

string

pri

Again, don't worry if you don't understand everything in this chart now. It's a useful list of things to try when you're debugging, so you can always refer back to it later.

Let's try a more complex program. This program will tell you how many days old you are. Just copy it into Python, then change the second line to have your birthday instead of mine. The first number is the year you were born, then the month of the year, then the day of the month. I was born on 22nd May 1986, so I've put

```
datetime.datetime(1986,5,22)
```

Don't forget to press Enter or Return at the end of each line!

```
>>> import datetime
>>> birthday = datetime.datetime(1986,5,22)
>>> today = datetime.datetime.now()
>>> number = (today - birthday).days
>>> print("You are", number, "days old")
```

28

The terminal should look something like this:

```
>>> import datetime
>>> birthday = datetime.datetime(1986,5,22)
>>> today = datetime.datetime.now()
>>> number = (today - birthday).days
>>> print("You are", number, "days old")
You are 10553 days old
```

Now you know the basics of how Python and Scratch work, it's time to get started with cool programming topic number one: dealing with data and variables!

loop

ariable

Imagine you wrote the number 7 on a piece of paper, then put the piece of paper in an envelope with `my_favourite_number` written on it. I agree to look after the envelope for you.

That's how variables work when you're writing code. A variable has a **name**, like `my_favourite_number` and a **value** like the number 7.

If you came back later and asked me what `my_favourite_number` was, I'd look in the envelope and show you the piece of paper with a 7 written on it.

That's how variables work in code too. You can use the name of a variable to use the value inside it. That way, if I want to find the number that's double my favourite number, I can tell the computer to take `my_favourite_number` and multiply it by two.

If you changed your mind and decided your favourite number was now 10, you could write that on a piece of paper and give it to me to put in the envelope. I would take out the old piece of paper and throw it in the recycling bin, and put the new piece of paper with 10 on it in the envelope instead. Now when you ask me for `my_favourite_number` I'll be able to show you it's 10, not 7.

That's the reason why variables are useful, because you can change the **value** that's stored inside a variable, but refer to it with the same **name**, and the computer will use the last **value** you gave it. Variables let us write code using values that might change, or where we can't know the value at the time we're writing the code.

For example, let's imagine writing a program that would double whatever number a user typed in. At the time when you're writing the code, you don't know what number the user will type. What you would need to do instead is to take the number they type, store it in a variable, and then double the variable.

In Python

In Python, variables are normally written with all lower-case words, separated with underscores _. This is something all Python coders do, because it makes it easier for us all to read and understand each other's code. We have to use underscores instead of spaces because in Python, variable names can't have spaces. On most computers you can type an underscore by pressing Shift with the - button.

To put a value into a variable, you always first write the variable's name, then an equals sign, then the value. Python will take everything on the right side of the equals sign, and then put it into the variable on the left side. This works even if you're replacing an existing value. For example, try typing in the code on the next page. Remember to press Enter at the end of each line.

You only need to type the lines that start with
>>>
All the other lines are Python telling you the result of
what you've just done.

```
>>> my_favourite_number = 7
>>> print(my_favourite_number)
7
>>> my_favourite_number = 10
>>> print(my_favourite_number)
10
>>> favourite_colour = "blue"
>>> print(favourite_colour)
blue
```

Remember: blue is inside quotation marks so that Python knows it's a string, not a command. (See page 47 for more on strings.)

To use the **value** from inside a variable, you just use the variable's name. Let's try it out with this code that will tell you the number of children in a class:

```
>>> number_of_girls = 9
>>> number_of_boys = 7
>>> print(number_of_boys + number_of_girls)
16
```

What's really clever is that you can use the value of one variable to make the value of another variable, for example in this code that works out how many black keys there are on a piano.

```
>>> keys_on_a_piano = 88
>>> white_keys = 52
>>> black_keys = keys_on_a_piano - white_keys
>>> print (black_keys)
36
```

The last line of code tells Python to take the number of keys on a piano (88), subtract the number of white keys (52), and store the answer (36) inside the variable `black_keys`.

 In Python, * is used to do multiplication and / is used to do division. + and - are for addition and subtraction.

Variables are useful because they help us with maths, and let us store answers that we might need lots of times in the rest of our code without having to do lots of calculations every time. When you refresh the page (or close it and open it again), Python will be reset and will forget all of your stored variables. It's a good idea to refresh the page when you start a new project, to reset Python and clear your screen.

Python Puzzle Part 1

It had been Charlie who dared Aisha to go inside Python Manor — the almost-certainly haunted house on the hill above town. Aisha never said no to a dare and now it looked like she might be in serious trouble. It had been at least 15 minutes since she'd disappeared through the creaking old door. "Come on," said Mia, "she's probably just messing around. Let's go after her." Finn followed, muttering, "There's no such thing as ghosts, there's no such thing as ghosts…" Charlie didn't want to be left on his own, so he ran to join them, just as they stepped inside. His jaw dropped. Python Manor was a crumbling old mansion from the outside. But inside, it was like stepping into the future! Everything was sleek and modern. Touchscreen computers lined the walls, green lights flashing.

"Wow!" said Charlie, awed. "This place is like a spaceship!"
"Come on" said Finn. "Let's find Aisha and get out of here. I don't want to get caught."

"TOO LATE!", a loud voice boomed. One of the screens lit up, and a video started. "It's Aisha!", gasped Mia. They saw Aisha creep into the house and look around in awe before suddenly disappearing through the floor! The video cut to an underground room where Aisha was banging on the door, shouting. She was trapped!

"Strangers aren't welcome here," the voice continued. "Your friend learnt that with a bump. You'll need to puzzle your way through five rooms to reach her. Try if you want, but at your own risk."

The video stopped and a metal door slid open silently.

"We're never going to get Aisha out," said Charlie. "It's hopeless!"

"We've got to at least try," said Mia, crossly. "Let's take a look at the first puzzle."

The children ran through the open doorway and saw the locked door on the other side of the room. There was a keypad on the door, and a screen above it displaying the words: *ENTER PASSCODE HERE*.

A second computer screen displayed the following message:

The passcode can be found from my age multiplied by itself, multiplied by the coordinates of the manor, and added to the number of pigeons living in the manor.

My age: 31
Coordinates of the manor: 128467
Number of pigeons: 2

"Oh no!" said Charlie. "How are we ever going to work it out?" Finn looked closer at the screen in front of them and saw the familiar flashing `>>>`.

"It's Python!", he cried. "We have to use Python to work out the answer." "Of course!", said Mia. "Okay, I think we just need to create variables called age, coordinates_of_manor and number_of_pigeons with the values we've been given."

"Brilliant", said Finn. "Then we just multiply age by age, then by coordinates_of_manor, and then add number_of_pigeons."

"I'll do it!", shouted Charlie. "Remember to press Enter between each line of code," Mia reminded him.

Can you beat them to it and use Python to work out what the passcode is?

PASSCODE: _____

> **Hint:** Type the following lines into Python, filling in the gaps
> as you go. Then turn to page 127 to check the answers.
>
> ```
> >>> age = _____
> >>> coordinates_of_manor = _____
> >>> number_of_pigeons = _____
> >>> passcode = age * _____ * _____ + _____
> >>> print(passcode)
> ```

"We've got it!" shouted Charlie. "Quickly, type it into the keypad and see if it works." Finn rushed over to the door and typed their answer into the keypad. It worked! The door slid open with a hiss and they hurried through. "One down, four to go" said Mia with a grin.

In this chapter, you've learned how to set variables in Python, and use them to do sums. To practise using variables, here are a few more questions to solve. See pages 127–128 for the answers.

1. Can you use variables to calculate how many seconds there are in a day?

> **Hint:** First of all, create a variable called **seconds_in_an_hour**, with a value of **60 * 60**. Next create a variable called **seconds_in_a_day** – the value of this should be **seconds_in_an_hour * 24** (remember, there are 24 hours in a day).

2. Here is a famous riddle called "As I was going to St Ives":

As I was going to St. Ives,
I met a man with seven wives,
Each wife had seven sacks,
Each sack had seven cats,
Each cat had seven kits:
Kits, cats, sacks, and wives,
How many were there going to St. Ives?

a) Can you use Python to work out how many kits (which is an old word for kittens) there are in the poem? It might help to work out how many sacks there are, then how many cats, then how many kits, putting each in a new variable. You'll need to use * for multiplication a lot!

> **Hint:** First of all, create a variable called **wives**, holding the number 7. Then, create a variable called **sacks**, the value of which should be **wives** multiplied by 7. Now do the same thing for **cats** and **kits**.

b) Can you work out the answer to the question at the end too: how many were going to St. Ives? The final answer to this should be:

```
>>> 1 + wives + sacks + cats + kits
```

In Scratch

You can see all of Scratch's blocks for using variables by clicking on the Data option in the block palette. We're going to create a new variable called "example variable". To do that, first create a new variable by clicking on the "Make a Variable" button. Next, type "example variable" into the "Variable name" box. You can leave the other settings alone for now ("For all sprites" should already be selected) and click "OK".

In Scratch, you can use spaces in the names of your variables, like "my favourite number", but in Python, you should use underscores instead, like this:
`my_favourite_number`

Once you've done that, you can see all the options Scratch gives you for using variables. There's a block with rounded corners that

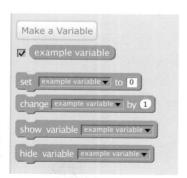

lets you use the value of the variable inside other blocks, a block that lets you set the value of the variable and a block that lets you change the value of a variable. There are two other blocks that let you show or hide the little box that shows the current value of the variable if you want to.

Let's have a look at how to use variables in Scratch!

Variables in Scratch

1. Let's make a program that can tell you about the number of monkeys and elephants in a zoo. We'll start by creating variables for the number of monkeys and the number of elephants. To do that, open the Data palette and click on "Make a Variable". When you're asked for the name of your variable, type "monkeys" into the box and click "OK" (you don't need to change the "For all sprites" setting). Then do the same thing again, but call this variable "elephants".

2. Now, let's set the number of elephants to 5, and the number of monkeys to 3 when the green flag is clicked. To do that, drag the "when green flag clicked" block from the Events palette into the scripts area. Then underneath it, drag the "set elephants to 0" block from the Data palette, but change the block to say "set elephants to 5". Now drag another identical "set elephants to 0" block underneath it, but change this one to say "set monkeys to 3".

3. The zoo is now given 4 more elephants and 2 more monkeys, so we should include that in the calculation by increasing the number of elephants by 4 and the number of monkeys by 2. From the Data palette, drag the "change elephants by 1" block underneath the last block, and change it to say "change elephants by 4". Now drag another identical block underneath, and change that to say "change monkeys by 2".

4. The last thing we should do is to work out how many animals are in the zoo in total. Let's create a new variable called "all animals", by clicking on "Make a Variable" in the Data palette. We need to set its value to be the number of monkeys + the number of elephants, so start by dragging a "set all animals to 0" block underneath the "change monkeys by 2". Now from the Operators palette, drag a "0+0" block onto the 0, so that the block says "set all animals to 0+0". Inside the two "0"s on the "0+0" block, drag the "elephants" and "monkeys" blocks from the Data palette.

5. Now when you run the program, you should see that you've correctly told Scratch how to calculate the number of animals in the zoo. If you've done this right, the value of the elephants variable (the number of elephants in your zoo) should be 9, the number of monkeys should be 5, and the number of all animals should be 14.

monkeys   5

elephants   9

all animals   14

Scratch Project 1

We're going to use variables to make the Scratch cat have a conversation with us!

1. First of all, the cat is going to say hello and ask how old you are. So when the green flag is clicked, the cat should say "Hello!" for 2 seconds, then ask for your age.

a) To start with, find the "when green flag clicked" block in the Events palette and drag that into the scripts area.

b) Next, find the "say Hello! for 2 secs" block in the Looks palette and drag that underneath the green flag block, so it slots into place.

c) Now, find the block that says "ask What's your name? and wait", which is in the Sensing palette. Drag the block so that it sticks to the bottom of the "say Hello! for 2 secs" block. At the moment the block asks for your name, but we want it to ask for your age instead, so let's change the question it asks. Delete the text where it says "What's your name?" and instead type "How old are you?"

d) Let's try what we have so far by clicking on the green flag above the stage area. The cat should say "Hello!", and then say "How old are you?", and a little blue box will appear at the bottom of the stage area. You can then type your age into the blue box and click on the tick when you've finished typing.

2. Now we're going to need to store the answer to that question somewhere, so that Scratch remembers it for us to use later.

a) First, go to the Data palette, and click "Make a Variable". We're going to call our variable "age". Again, just leave "For all sprites" selected and click OK.

b) The next step is to tell Scratch that what we typed in the blue box should be stored in the variable age. Look under the Data palette, and you'll find a block for "set age to 0". This will set the value of our age variable to 0, which is close to what we need it to do, so drag that underneath the "ask How old are you? and wait" block.

c) Now we need to change that last block a bit, because we don't want to set age to 0, we want to set it to what was typed in. Go to the Sensing palette and find the small block that says "answer". This block is a variable where Scratch stores the last thing that was typed into our program. Drag this "answer" block to replace the 0 in the "set age to 0" block, so that it says "set age to answer".

d) Let's try what we've made so far to check that it works. Click on the green flag above the stage and type in your age when you're asked for it. Scratch will show you what value is currently stored in the "age" variable inside a small box in the stage area. You should see it change when you type in your answer.

3. Next, we'll make Scratch do something clever! First of all the cat will say "That's a great age! In one year, you'll be…" and then it'll tell you how old you'll be this time next year.

a) The first part of this can be done by taking another "say Hello! for 2 secs" block from the Looks palette, putting it underneath the "set age to answer" block, and changing the "Hello!" text to "That's a great age! In one year you'll be…".

b) The next step is for the cat to say how old you'll be next year. In one year's time, your age will be whatever your current age is, plus one. So the cat should say whatever is in the "age" variable, plus one. Let's take another "say Hello! for 2 secs" block and change the "Hello!" to be the value of name + 1. To do this, take the "O + O" block from the Operators palette and drag it into the "Hello!" part of the block. Then drag the "age" variable from the Data palette into the first "O" of the block, then click in the second "O" and type the number 1.

c) Now try your conversation with the cat again. It should look something like this:

```
when ⚑ clicked
say Hello! for 2 secs
ask How old are you ? and wait
set age ▾ to answer
say That's a great age! In one year you'll be… for 2 secs
say age + 1 for 2 secs
```

You've just made a program that talks to the user, asks them their age, and can tell them how old they'll be next year. This Scratch code shows why variables are so useful. If you run your program again, and put in the age of someone else, Scratch will be able to tell you how old they'll be next year. And you don't have to change the code at all! If you hadn't used a variable, you'd have had to change the code to give different results for different ages.

Take it further...

1. The cat could help you with some maths. Change the code we wrote above to make the cat ask for a number (instead of your age) and store it in a variable called "number 1". Then make the cat ask for another number, and store that in a variable called "number 2". Now, instead of telling you your age next year, can you make the cat tell you what you get when you multiply the two numbers together?

   Hint: you'll need to use the "O * O" block in the Operators palette for this.

2. Can you make the cat meow every time it asks a question?

   Hint: you can find the "play sound meow" block in the Sound palette.

You'll find the answers on page 128.

In this chapter, you've learned what variables are, and how they let you write your code once but run it lots of times and give different results. You've also learned how useful they can be for storing answers that you need to use later in your code (like the number of cats in the St. Ives poem). Why not try out your Scratch project on your family and friends? Get them to enter their age to find out how old they'll be next year, or use your multiplication program to wow them with your maths skills!

CHAPTER 2: TYPES
ABC, easy as 123

In Python

If I told you to add 2 and 3, you'd get 5. But if I told you to add "I like" and "cookies", you'd end up with "I like cookies". You can do exactly the same in code. If you go to the Python window and type:

```
>>> 2 + 3
```

and press Enter, Python will tell you the answer is `5`. If you try typing:

```
>>> "I like" + "cookies"
```

Python will tell you the answer is `'I likecookies'`.

How does Python know to add the two numbers together to get 5, but to join the words into a sentence? And why doesn't it know to put a space in between "like" and "cookies"?

The answer is because coding uses types. A type tells you what sort of thing you have – like a number or a word. Two of the most common types are integers and strings.

An integer means a whole number like 1, 2, 20, 0, -1 and -1000. In Python, the word integer is shortened to int. When you tell Python to do `2 + 3`, it knows that you mean "take the number 2 and add it to the number 3". So it gives you the result, `5`, which is another integer.

Remember: you already learned how to subtract, multiply, add
and divide integers using -, *, + and / (see page 33).

A string can be a single letter, a word, spaces or even whole
sentences. In Python, string is shortened to str. Strings in Python
are always surrounded by speech marks or quotes like this:

```
>>> "This is a string."
>>> "And so is this!"
>>> "Strings can contain numbers like 101"
```

When you tell Python to add two strings together with the + sign, it
will join the strings together into a longer string. But it won't put in
spaces for you – you have to tell Python where the spaces should be
by putting them inside the string. So

```
>>> "My" + "name" + "is" + "Python"
```
gives
```
'MynameisPython'
```
But
```
>>> "My " + "name " + "is " + "Python"
```
gives
```
'My name is Python'
```
So what do you think you'll get if you tell Python to do
```
>>> "2" + "3"
```
?
Try it now.

You might have thought that you would get 5. But because the
2 and 3 are inside speech marks, Python will interpret them as
strings, and will join them together to give `'23'`, as it would with
any other strings.

Combining types

Try asking Python to do

```
>>> "2" + 4
```

What do you see?

When you try to add "2" and 4, Python gives an error message because "2" is a string and 4 is an integer, and it doesn't know how to add them together because they're different types.

There are two ways we can fix this. If we want Python to add them together as numbers, we can tell Python to convert "2" into an integer first, which we can do by typing `int(` then the thing we want to convert, which is `"2"` then the final `)`

So we would type:
```
>>> int("2") + 4
```

Try it now. You should find that Python gives the answer 6.

Strings are one of the most important types of data because almost everything can be made into a string. Names are strings, like "Python"; dates can be strings, like "1st January"; and numbers can be strings, like "100". When our program gets input from someone typing, Python will receive that as a string, because strings can be used to represent lots of different types of data. It's then up to us as coders to convert those strings to different types if we need to. (See page 74 for more on input.)

For example, you might write a program that knows there are 2 children in a classroom, and then asks the user how many more children come in. If the user enters 4, that will be interpreted as a string inside Python, not a number. To calculate how many children are now in the classroom, your code will need to convert the 4 into an integer before Python can do the addition.

But, if we want Python to join them together as strings instead, we can tell Python to convert 4 to a string first, which we do by typing `str(` then the thing we want to convert, which is `4` then the final `)`

So we would type:

```
>>> "2" + str(4)
```

Try it now. You should find that Python gives the answer "24". This is useful for joining numbers together, rather than adding them up.

When might we want to convert a number into a string? Quite often! Every time your code has a variable with a number, and you want to use it in a sentence, it has to be converted to a string. For example, if your code worked out that the temperature (in degrees Celsius) was 25, and you wanted to output "The temperature today is 25°C", you would first need to convert the 25 from a number to a string.

Mia, Finn and Charlie raced into the next room and looked around. There was a single door on the other side – they rushed over to it. A screen on the door flashed the words: **ENTER PASSWORD HERE**. Below it was the following clue:

The password is a string, made by joining these three things together: my pet tortoise's age multiplied by 3, my favourite sweets and my favourite number.

Underneath that, the following code was displayed:

```
age = 59
age_times_three = age * 3
sweets = "toffees"
favourite_number = 13
password = _____ + _____ + _____
print(password)
```

"That's easy!" said Charlie. "We just need to add the variables." Finn and Mia looked at each other – surely it couldn't be that simple? Charlie typed the code into Python and pressed Enter. "It's not working!" he cried. "It just gives an error message. There must be a bug in the code. How are we supposed to work it out?"

"Let me see," said Mia, pushing Charlie to one side. "Aha! A classic mistake. This won't take a second to fix."

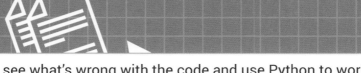

Can you see what's wrong with the code and use Python to work out the password before Mia does? See page 129 for the answer.

PASSWORD:_____

Hint: At the moment the password isn't working because it's trying to add numbers to strings. You might have to convert everything to strings first.

"Of course!" said Finn. "Okay, let's type it in and see if it works." Charlie entered the password into the computer and the door swung open. "We did it!" he grinned. "At this rate we'll have Aisha out in ..." Charlie trailed off. He had just caught sight of what the next room held, and it didn't look promising...

Did you notice that we used variables too? We couldn't just add the variables together because their values are a mixture of integers and strings, and we can't just mix the types. That's why we needed to convert the integers to strings.

Now you know how to use different types of variables in your code, when to use integer and string variables, and how to convert between them. To practise working with different types, here's another problem to solve:

Let's try to make a program that can write out the answer to difficult multiplication sums. You could make two variables called `number_1` and `number_2` for the numbers you want to multiply, and then put the answer to the multiplication in a variable called `answer`. The hard part is to use print() to tell someone the answer to the sum. So, if your numbers were 2 and 3, the final line of your code should say `"2 multiplied by 3 is 6"`. To do that, you'll need to convert `number_1`, `number_2` and `answer` into strings, then join them together with the words "multiplied by" and "is" between them.

Check that it works with bigger numbers too, for example setting `number_1` to 114 and `number_2` to 97 should print `'114 multiplied by 97 is 11058'`.

> **Hint:** Remember, to convert the variables to strings you'll need to type `str()`. For example, `str(number_1)`.

See page 129 for the answer.

In Scratch

Scratch also uses types. Create a new project, and drag the "Say Hello! for 2 secs" block from the Looks palette into the scripts area. Remember you can click on a block at any time to make Scratch run it, so try that with the block you just dragged now.

You've already used the "O+O" block from the Operators palette to add two numbers together. This time, drag it into the "Say Hello! for 2 secs" block to replace the word "Hello!". Now let's change it to say "2 + 3". Try clicking on the block: you should see the Scratch cat say "5" in the stage area.

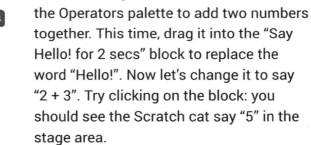

What happens if we try to make the cat to say "Easy as " + "ABC" instead? You can try typing it into the "O+O" block, but Scratch won't let you. That's because Scratch knows that the "O+O" block only works with numbers. If you want to join strings together, you have to use the "join" block instead.

Let's try that now. Drag the "O+O" block out of "Say O+O for 2 sec", and replace it with the "join hello world" block from the Operators palette.

Now, change the "join hello world" block to say "join Easy as ABC", and then click on it. The Scratch cat will say "Easy asABC". Just like Python, you have to remember to put in an extra space after the word "as" if you want the cat to say "Easy as ABC".

What do you think will happen if we change our "join Easy as ABC" block to say "join 2 3"? Try it now.

The Scratch cat should say "23" to you – just like when you added together the strings "2" and "3" in Python! Even though the two languages can look quite different, they work in a similar way.

Remember: In Python, the + sign is used for adding numbers and it's also used for joining strings, but if you try to add a number to a string, you'll get an error. In Scratch, you can use the "+" block to add two numbers but not strings. And you can use the "join" block to join together two strings but not to add numbers.

Scratch Project 2

For this project we're going to have another conversation with the Scratch cat. This time, we're going to join strings together so that the cat speaks in proper sentences.

1. First of all, the cat is going to say "Hello" for a couple of seconds, then ask "What's your name?" and wait.

2. Let's store the answer to that question in a new variable called "name", like we did before. Don't forget to set name to answer in your script.

3. Now the Scratch cat is going to reply saying "Hello " and then the person's name, and then ask how they are. In Scratch, you have to use "join" to put two strings together, and you have to use "+" to add two numbers, so you have to decide whether you're joining or adding to know which block to use. This is different from Python, where you write both in the same way (with a "+"), but you have to convert them to be strings for joining, or integers for adding. Here, we'll need "join", which is in the Operators palette. We need to join "Hello " and the "name" variable, and then put that inside the "Say hello for 2 secs" block. Next, we'll use the "ask What's your name? and wait" block again, but this time we'll use it to ask "How are you feeling?"

4. Whatever the person says, we'll store their answer in a new variable called "mood". As before, don't forget to set mood to answer in your script.

5. Lastly, the Scratch cat is going to reply saying that he is feeling the same as you, by joining "I also feel " with the variable "mood".

Click on your script to try the conversation! Ask other people to try it, too.

In most Scratch we've done until now, we've put the "when green flag clicked" event block at the beginning of our scripts. It's a good habit to get into when your scripts get more complicated, but you don't need to begin every script with a "when green flag clicked". Whether or not you begin a script with a "when green flag clicked", you can always run the script just by clicking on it.

Take it further...

1. Can you make the Scratch cat make a "meow" noise every time he speaks?

   Hint: you'll need to use the "play sound meow" block from the Sounds palette.

2. How about making the cat bigger every time he asks a question, so it feels like he's walking towards you?

   Hint: you'll need to use the "change size by 10" block from the Looks palette. What difference does it make if you change that 10 to 1, then run the script? What about if you change the 10 to a 30?

You'll find the answers on page 130.

⊚ CHAPTER 3: LOOPS ⊚
Around and around

It can be really boring to do the same thing again and again, like washing dishes or putting socks into pairs. Luckily for us, as well as being stupid, computers never get bored. So if we tell them to do something over and over, they'll just do it without complaining (unlike when you get asked to tidy your room!).

One of the easiest ways of telling a computer to do something repeatedly is to use loops. For example, an algorithm for making three slices of toast could be written as:

1. **Put a slice of bread in the toaster**
2. **Push the lever down to turn on the toaster**
3. **Remove the toasted bread from the toaster**
4. **Put a slice of bread in the toaster**
5. **Push the lever down to turn on the toaster**
6. **Remove the toasted bread from the toaster**
7. **Put a slice of bread in the toaster**
8. **Push the lever down to turn on the toaster**
9. **Remove the toasted bread from the toaster**

If we use a loop, it's much simpler.

1. **Do the following 3 steps, 3 times:**
   a) **Put a slice of bread in the toaster**
   b) **Push the lever down to turn on the toaster**
   c) **Remove the toasted bread from the toaster**

It's much faster to type, and easier to read. This kind of loop tells the computer to do the same thing a set number of times but programs can use loops for lots of different things:

- Games use loops to repeatedly change what's shown on the screen.
- Websites use loops to show groups of things that look similar but have different text in them (like the comments under a YouTube video).

In Python

Let's get Python to say "Hip hip hooray!" three times. Try typing the code below into Python.

- Remember to type the `:` at the end of the first line!
- You don't need to type the `...` – Python will automatically change the prompt from `>>>` to `...` because it's waiting for you to type more code.
- When you type the second line, make sure you type four spaces before you type `print("Hip hip hooray!")`.
- Make sure you leave the third line blank, and just press Enter.

```
>>> for number in range(3):
...     print("Hip hip hooray!")
...
Hip hip hooray!
Hip hip hooray!
Hip hip hooray!
```

The first line here is what tells Python to do a loop. The `for` keyword tells Python to do a loop, and `number` is a variable name that we can choose. Each time through the loop, Python will put a new value in this variable.

The second line is the code we want Python to loop over. The four spaces at the start of the line are an **indent** which you have to include so Python can tell which code should be looped over.

The blank line at the end, where we just pressed Enter, tells Python that the loop has finished. You can put more than one line of code inside the loop, as long as you remember to type the blank spaces at the start for the indent. Python will wait until you type a blank line so that it knows the loop is finished, then run your code.

Let's try this experiment to see what value the variable holds each time through the loop (don't forget to type the : and the four spaces for the indent):

```
>>> for number in range(3):
...     print(number)
...
```

Remember that `print()` tells Python to write something out onto the console. In this case, it'll write out the value that's inside the variable called number.

If you run this code, you should see output like this:

```
0
1
2
```

As you'd expect, there are three numbers here, but surprisingly they're 0–2 not 1–3. It's very common in programming to start counting from 0, instead of 1. But the code will still count through three numbers, whatever number it starts from.

Because number is a variable name that we chose, we could give it any other name and Python would still produce the same output.

Try it below, and don't forget the : and indent!

```
>>> for sausage in range(3):
...      print(sausage)
...
```

The `in` gives Python the list of things we'd like it to loop through, which is generated by `range(3)` which tells Python to loop through three numbers (0, 1 and 2).

If you want Python to count up to 5, you should use `range(6)` which tells Python to loop through 0, 1, 2, 3, 4, 5.

The : tells Python that the next lines will be indented, and that we want Python to run those lines each time it goes through the loop. It's very important to write this in, otherwise Python will fail with a "Syntax Error" – meaning that it didn't understand what you were asking it to do.

The second line looks a lot like things we've seen before, but with four extra spaces (or an indent) at the start. It's very important to remember these spaces too, so that Python knows which things should be looped, and where the loop ends. The lines which start with four extra spaces are the things that Python will loop over. The first blank line is the end of the loop. You probably noticed that the lines that are looped begin with ... instead of >>>.

That's Python's way of telling you that you can add more indented lines of code to the loop. The extra blank line you have to type afterwards tells Python that the loop has ended. Python will wait until it knows the loop has ended before running your code.

For example, let's try to make Python say:
Hi ho!
Hi ho!
It's off to work we go!

Try typing this:

```
>>> for anything in range(2):
...     print("Hi ho!")
...
>>> print("It's off to work we go!")
```

As soon as you type the blank third line, Python will print "Hi ho!" twice, because it knows the loop is finished. But "It's off to work we go!" is outside the loop because it isn't indented, so it will only be printed once. You should end up with code that looks like this:

```
>>> for anything in range(2):
...     print("Hi ho!")
...
Hi ho!
Hi ho!
>>> print("It's off to work we go!")
It's off to work we go!
```

Python Puzzle Part 3

"Oh no!", Charlie stopped in his tracks. "Wow!", said Mia, coming in behind him and seeing what lay ahead. What they could see was an enormous room with a wall of doors stretching off into the distance. "There could be hundreds of doors in here – how on earth are we going to work out which is the right one to go through?", said Charlie.

The children looked more closely at the doors. They tried to open a few, but none of them would budge. Each door was numbered, starting from 0. "I'll run to the end of the room and see what number it goes up to," said Finn. And he sprinted off down the long room. In a moment he was back, panting: "99. It goes up to 99 and starts at 0, so there must be exactly 100 doors."

At that moment, Finn spotted a clue flashing on a screen in the wall next to them:

To find the right door, take its number and multiply it by the number of the next door along. If you get 4556, you've found the right door.

"Okay, let's start with door 1," Finn suggested. "The next door along is 2, so we have to multiply 1 by 2, which is 2. The next door along is 3, and 2 times 3 is 6. Next is..."

"Stop! That's going to take forever. There must be a better way," said Mia, thinking fast. "Listen, I think we can use Python to quickly loop through all the numbers between 0 and 99, and find out what the multiplication would come to!"

Can you use Python to loop through the numbers and work out which door they should go through?

CORRECT DOOR: _____

Hint: Try filling in the gaps here:

```
>>> for door in range (_____):
...     print("door number")
...     print(door)
...     print("Answer is")
...     print(_____ * (_____ + 1))
...
```

This should give you a list of answers for each door number. And one of the door numbers will give you the answer 4556. Turn to page 131 to check your answer.

"Got it!" shouted Mia. "Follow me." The three of them ran towards the door with the number Mia had found and turned the handle. It opened! On the other side, a flight of stairs led down into darkness. "We must be getting closer to the basement where Aisha is," said Finn. Taking a deep breath, Finn led the way down the stairs into the blackness below...

Changing Variables

So far, you've learned two ways of using variables in Python. The first one sets a variable to a value, like:

```
feet_on_a_dog = 4
```

The second one uses the value stored in a variable, like:

```
print(secret_code)
```

But there's also a third way to use variables, where we use the same variable twice in the same line of code, like:

```
skill_level = skill_level + 1
```

This line of code will add 1 to the value of skill_level, then put that back in the variable called skill_level. This might seem odd at first, but it'll make more sense if you think of the computer as doing the right-hand side of the "=" first then putting that in the variable on the left side of the "=".

What do you think each of these would do?

```
1. number_of_lives = number_of_lives
   - 1
```

```
2. answer = str(answer)
```

```
3. points = points * 10
```

See page 131 for the answers.

Now that you've mastered loops in Python, try these challenges to practise them some more. The answers are on page 131–132.

1. Get Python to help with your 7 times table! Write a loop that goes from 0 up to 12, using a variable called number. Every time through the loop, tell Python to write out 7 multiplied by number. Try it with other times tables too!

> **Hint:** Fill in the gaps here. Remember that loops in Python go up to 1 less than the number you put in range.

```
>>> for number in range (_____):
...        answer = 7*_____
...        print("7 times " + str(_____) + " is "
+ str(_____))
...
```

2. What do you get if you add together all of the numbers from 0 to 999? See if you can get Python to tell you!

> **Hint:** First, make sure you've read about changing variables (see opposite), then fill in the gaps here:

```
>>> total = 0
>>> for number in range (_____):
...        total = _____ + _____
...        print(total)
...
```

Remember that Python will only loop the lines that are indented inside the loop. So even though total is set to 0 at the beginning, each time through the loop will add to total.

In Scratch

Scratch's loops can be found in the Control section of the block palette. The one we're going to use is the one with "repeat 10" showing. We can change the number of repetitions by clicking on the 10 and typing in a new number.

The blocks that Scratch will run multiple times in a loop are all the ones that are held within the yellow repeat block, up to the arrow. That could be just one block, or it might be loads of blocks. Scratch has other types of loop too, like the "forever" loop, which will keep running the same blocks again and again, until you press the red stop button.

So, let's take the same example again of singing "Hi ho! Hi ho! It's off to work we go!". First take a "repeat 10" block from the Control palette, and change the 10 to a 2.

Then drag a "say Hello! for 2 secs" block inside the repeat block, and change the "Hello!" to "Hi ho!". Now drag a "wait 1 secs" block from the Control palette and drop it in between the "say Hi ho! for 2 secs block" and the bottom of the "repeat 2" block.

Finally, after the repeat block, drag another "say Hello! for 2 secs" block, but this time change the "Hello!" to say "It's off to work we go!".

Remember you can click on the blocks at any time to try the script out. You should see the cat say "Hi ho!" for 2 seconds, stop for 1 second, then say "Hi ho!" again for 2 seconds, then stop for 1 second, then say "It's off to work we go!" for 2 seconds.

Scratch Project 3

Let's use loops to make our cat dance. We'll also choose some drums to play in the background. But how shall we decide which drums to play? And should the cat do big or little dance steps? We can use variables to try the different options, and loops to make the cat keep on dancing!

1. Let's start by creating two variables that will let us change the drums and how big the cat's dance is (remember, you can find variables in the Data palette). We'll call our two variables "dance size" and "drum type". It's fine to leave the variable box set to "For all sprites". As soon as you've created the variables, you should see two boxes appear with their name and their value in the stage area. If you double-click twice on each box, they'll change to having a slider underneath, which will make it much easier to change the values.

2. Now, let's start with the animation. When the flag is clicked, we want to make the cat do the same dance moves 16 times. To do that, start by taking a "repeat 10" block from the Control palette, then change the 10 to 16. Everything that goes inside the repeat block will be done 16 times, so that's where we'll put all of the dance steps for the cat to follow.

3. First of all, we want the cat to move when it dances. How far do we want it to move? Well that depends on the value of the "dance size" variable. Drag the "change x by 10" and "change y by 10" blocks from the Motion palette, and drop them both inside the loop block. Then

drag the "dance size" variable into both of the Motion blocks so that they say "change x by dance size" and "change y by dance size".

It's sometimes useful to know a little bit of maths when programming, particularly for graphs. All you need to know here is that "x" is used to mean how far something is across from the left side, and "y" means how far something is up from the bottom of the graph. If you find it hard to remember this, just remember that the letter x is a cross shape – "x is across!". Adding to the "x" value of something will move it to the right, but adding to the "y" value of something will move it up. Setting the "x" and "y" values to 0 will move it back to where it started.

4. Now that the cat has moved a bit, we're going to add a drum noise to go with it. But which drum noise? Let's use our new variable! Take the "play drum 1 for 0.25 beats" block from the Sounds palette and put it inside the loop after both of the Motion blocks you just added.

Next, drag the "drum type" variable into the box so that it says "play drum drum type for 0.25 beats". Now the drum that plays will change whenever we change the "drum type" variable.

```
when [flag] clicked
repeat 16
    change x by (dance size)
    change y by (dance size)
    play drum (drum type) for (0.25) beats
```

5. No disco is complete without some flashing coloured lights, so let's change the colour of the cat too. Find the "change color effect by 25" block in the Looks palette, and drag that inside the loop, after the "play drum" block. Change the 25 to 20.

```
when [flag] clicked
repeat 16
    change x by (dance size)
    change y by (dance size)
    play drum (drum type) for (0.25) beats
    change color effect by 20
```

6. When the cat has moved, played the drum and changed colour, we should bring it back to where it started from by setting the x and y values to 0, and playing a different drum. To do that, drag a "go to x:0 y:0" block from the Motion palette, and add it to the bottom

```
when [flag] clicked
repeat 16
    change x by (dance size)
    change y by (dance size)
    play drum (drum type) for (0.25) beats
    change color effect by 20
    go to x: 0 y: 0
    play drum 8 for (0.25) beats
```

of your script. The block might say other numbers to start with, like "go to x:123 y:-92", so change them both to 0. Then drag a "play drum 1 for 0.25 beats" block from the Sound block to the bottom of the script. We don't want all of our drum sounds to be the same, so this time let's play drum 8 for 0.25 seconds.

Because we haven't used the "drum type" variable, the drum sound that is played won't change when we change our variable.

7. We've now created a dance for the cat to do when the green flag is clicked, and we should be able to change the size of the dance, and the first drum beat that's heard by changing the value of the two variables. Let's try that now — click on the green flag and you should start hearing drum noises. While the cat is still dancing, try sliding the sliders for the dance size and drum type variables to see how that changes the way the cat dances.

8. Let's try one more thing. There are actually only 18 different drum types but the slider goes up to 100, which makes it quite hard to try the different drum types. Instead of using the slider, let's make it so that when we click on the cat sprite, we start using the next drum type. To do that, we're going to make a second script in the scripts area. This script will start with the "when this sprite clicked" block from the Events palette. Drag it into the scripts area next to, but not joined onto, the script we've already made for making the cat dance. When we click the cat, we want to change the drum

```
when 🏴 clicked
repeat 16
    change x by (dance size)
    change y by (dance size)
    play drum (drum type) for (0.25) beats
    change color effect by 20
    go to x: 0 y: 0
    play drum 8▾ for 0.25 beats
```

```
when this sprite is clicked
change drum type ▾ by 1
```

type by 1. You'll need to use a block from the Data palette for that, by dragging it underneath the "when this sprite clicked" block.

So now our cat will do 16 dance steps of the size we tell it, and will use a different drum noise when we click on it. You should see the drum type slider go up by 1 whenever you click the cat. Try it out!

Take it further...

If you get stuck, turn to page 132 for the answers.

1. Can you make the cat dance faster whenever it's clicked? You'll need to use the "change tempo by 20" block from the Sound palette. (If you want to reset the tempo back down to 60 at any point, just click on the "set tempo to 60 bpm" block in the Sound palette.)

2. Try adding music as well! With the "when space key is pressed" block from the Events palette and the "play note 60 for 0.5 beats" block from the Sound palette, you can make keys on your keyboard play musical notes! By having 5 of each block, with each "when space key is pressed" joining onto a "play note 60 for 0.5 beats", you can play lots of different notes. I recommend changing the blocks so that your "a" key plays note 60, your "s" plays note 62, your "d" plays note 64, your "f" key plays note 65 and your "g" plays note 67. See what music you can create by typing a, s, d, f and g!

CHAPTER 4: INPUT
Giving your program eyes and ears

Input lets our programs respond to us. It's how we can give our programs eyes and ears!

If you think about some of the objects around a house, they have lots of different kinds of input. A microwave has buttons so you can enter a length of time, a toaster has a dial you can turn to change how long it spends toasting your bread.

In coding, **input** means any data that comes from outside your program. That includes data downloaded from a webpage on the Internet, or from a file on your computer. But the inputs you'll use most of the time are from people typing things on a keyboard or pointing and clicking a mouse. Coders might use these so that your character in a game moves around when you press certain buttons, or to decide what happens when you click on a link on a webpage. Let's see how you can use them!

In Python

Python makes it really easy to get input from the keyboard that we can use in our programs. For example, if we want to ask for the name of the person using our program, we would write this code:

```
>>> name = input("What is your name? ")
```

(Make sure you include the brackets and the extra space at the end.) Getting input like this tells Python to ask "What is your name? ". It will then wait for you to type something and press Enter. The extra space is there so that there's a gap between the question Python asks and the answer that you type. When it has received the input, it will store it in a variable called name.

 Remember, on some computers the Enter key is called the Return key, or has an icon like this: ↵

Try this program to see it in action. Make sure you include the spaces after "name?" and "Hi", so that Python leaves spaces when you join the strings together.

```
>>> name = input("What is your name? ")
>>> print("Hi " + name + "!")
```

This will ask you what your name is and wait for you to type something. If you type in "Zoe" and press Enter, then Python will say "Hi Zoe!". The last line of code works by adding the string "Hi " to the name you typed in, and then adding a "!" at the end.

When Python gets input, it's always as a string. So if you want to use input as numbers, you have to convert its type (see page 46 for a reminder on types). Let's try that now. After you type the first line, Python will say "What number should I double?", then wait for you to type in a number. You can type any number you want!

```
>>> number_string = input("What number should I double? ")
>>> number = int(number_string)
>>> doubled = 2*number
>>> print(doubled)
```

You've just created a doubling program! First of all, Python will ask for a number to be doubled. This goes into the variable called number_string. Remember – Python always gets input as a string.

The second line of code converts the string into an integer type, and stores that in the variable called number. The third line of code doubles the number and stores the result in a variable called doubled. The last line prints the answer onto the screen.

The doubling program you've written might be useful for making a calculator program, but it's just one example of using input in your programs. Input is used everywhere in programs that respond to users or files or websites. Without input, our programs would do exactly the same thing, with exactly the same results, every time they were run.

Combining Lines of Code

The code on page 76 does exactly the same thing as this code:

```
>>> number_string = input("What
number should I double? ")
>>> number = int(number_string)
>>> print(2*number)
```

The only difference is that we're not storing the doubled number in its own variable – we skipped that step and printed it straight onto the screen at the same time as we doubled it. In fact, we could also skip another line and do this:

```
>>> number_string = input("What
number should I double? ")
>>> print(2*int(number_string))
```

Remember how a variable is like an envelope with a value written inside it? Well, number was just an envelope for the value of int(number_string), so wherever we use the variable number, we could instead put int(number_string). This lets us write less code to get the same result.

To practise using input, have a go at writing these two programs:
1. Let's use Python to help work out what your name is backwards. You can try it out on all your friends, too. First of all, use input to ask for someone's name, and store it in a variable called name. Then store the backwards name in a variable called backwards_name. To do that, you'll need to get Python to reverse a string, which you can do by typing `name[::-1]`.

Hint: Fill in the gaps below.

```
>>> name = _____("What name shall I reverse? ")
>>> backwards_name = _____[::-1]
>>> print(_____)
```

2. You could also make a program which tells someone how many months old they are. First of all, use input to find out how old they are in years, then use input again to find out how many months since their last birthday. Store the answers in two variables called age_years and months_since_birthday. There are 12 months in a year, so at their last birthday, the person had lived for 12*age_years months. We need to add on months_since_birthday to get the final answer. But first, we'll need to convert the variables to numbers (remember Python gets all input as strings). Once you've converted the input to numbers using int(), you can calculate the final answer in a variable called months_old. Test it out on other people too!

Hint: Fill in the gaps here with the names of some of our variables, the word input, or the number 12:

```
>>> age_years = _____("How old are you? ")
>>> months_since_birthday = _____("How many months since your last birthday? ")
>>> months_old = _____*int(_____) + int(_____)
>>> print(_____)
```

See page 133 for the answers.

Python Puzzle Part 4

When Mia, Charlie and Finn reached the bottom of the staircase, they could see a few flashing lights, but it took a moment for their eyes to adjust to the darkness. With a shock, they realized that a shadowy figure was standing in front of a door. "What do we do?" whispered Charlie. Mia took a step forward, and tried to tiptoe silently around the figure. She was reaching slowly towards the door handle when suddenly something grabbed her hand tightly and bright lights flooded the room. A huge metal robot was gripping her arm and blocking the door!

Mia leapt backwards, and the robot let go of her hand. "Look, over here!" called Finn. A small screen next to the robot guard lit up with the following clue:

Every 5 seconds the robot will display a different number between 1 and a million. If you reply with the right passcode for that number, the robot guard will let you through. The passcode is found by multiplying the robot's number by 9, then subtracting 3.

If the robot says 202, you should reply with 1815 because 9*202 is 1818 and when you subtract 3 you get 1815. If the robot says 28101, you should say 252906 because 28101*9 is 252909 and when you subtract 3 you get 252906.

At that moment a screen on the robot began to flash numbers. Every 5 seconds, a new one appeared: *399756... 482... 700813... 2078... 652001... 1372...*

"The answer changes every 5 seconds!" wailed Charlie. "We'll never be able to keep up!" "And the numbers are too big! I don't see how we can do it in time," agreed Finn. "Of course we can!" said Mia. "Surely you've worked it out by now. We just need to use Python. If we use what the robot says as an input, we can find the answer really easily." With that, she began to enter her code into the computer.

Can you use Mia's clue to work out the right passcode for the last six numbers the robot displayed? See page 133 for the answers.

See page 133 for the answers.

PASSCODE FOR 399756: _____

PASSCODE FOR 482: _____

PASSCODE FOR 700813: _____

PASSCODE FOR 2078: _____

PASSCODE FOR 652001: _____

PASSCODE FOR 1372: _____

Hint: Mia's right about using the robot's number as an input. You can use a loop to run your code six times, and remember that inputs in Python are strings, so you'll have to convert it to an integer first. Try filling in the gaps here:

```
>>> for time in range(_):
...     robot_number = _____("What did the
robot say? ")
...     number = int(_____)
...     answer = _____*number - _____
...     print(answer)
```

"Quickly!" shouted Mia. "We've only got 2 seconds left. Type in the answer!" Charlie entered the last passcode into the robot as fast as he could. As soon as he pressed Enter, the robot lowered its arms, bowed its head and its lights went out. The children moved nervously past it, expecting it to wake up at any moment, but it didn't stir.

When they were through the door, they could hear a faint banging sound coming from the other side of the vast underground room. "Aisha!" said Finn. "That must be her we can hear!" The three of them ran as fast as they could towards the sound. "Don't worry, Aisha!" called Charlie. "We'll have you out any minute now."

"I wouldn't be so sure" said Mia, looking at the screen on the door...

Can you think of other ways to use input? You could write Python programs to help with your maths homework!

81

In Scratch

We've actually already used input in
Scratch before. For example, when we
were coding a conversation with the
cat, we used input when we used the
blue block "ask How old are you? and
wait". We then set our "age" variable to
be the answer that was typed in.

That's one way of using input in Scratch. When we want to get an
answer from the person using our code, we can use the "ask What's
your name? and wait" block from the Sensing palette. We can then
use a variable to store the answer.

Another way of getting input in Scratch
is with input **events**. Events let us tell
Scratch what we want it to do when the
user does something. So far, we've used
the event "when green flag clicked" a lot,
but we also used the "when this sprite
clicked" event to change the drum sound
when the cat was dancing, and one of
the extensions to the dance used the
"when space key pressed" event. All of those and more can be found
in the Events palette. As you've seen, they let us write code to be run
when a button is pressed on the keyboard, or when a button or sprite
is clicked. Remember, a sprite is a character or image, like the cat.

The difference between Sensing inputs (like the "ask What's your name? and wait" block) and Event inputs (like "when green flag clicked") is when we expect the input to happen. When Scratch runs the Sensing block, it will wait for input from the user and only carry on once the user has input something. These blocks are really useful for asking questions like "What's your name?" or asking the user to make decisions like "Where should we go next?" in a game.

With the Event blocks, Scratch will be ready to respond when a user presses a button on the keyboard, or clicks on the cat, and it will immediately run the code that goes with that event. This is useful for times when the user has to decide exactly what moment to do something, which might be in code for steering a car or swinging a tennis racquet. But because Event blocks wait for a single click or a single keyboard press, we can't use them for getting input of whole words or sentences – we have to use Sensing blocks for that.

Scratch Project 4

We're going to make a driving game! This will use some new parts of Scratch that we haven't used before.

The backdrop view is the place to change the backgrounds that show behind your sprites. You can choose a backdrop from the Scratch library, paint your own, upload a picture, or take a picture with your computer's camera (1).

The list on the left (2) shows all the backdrops you've made in your project, and you can click on a backdrop to edit it.

The main panel on the right (3) shows the backdrop you're currently editing.

The rectangle in the middle is the backdrop (4), and the tools on the left (5) let you draw with a paintbrush, draw straight lines, rectangles, circles and ellipses, write text, fill an area with a colour, erase bits of your drawing, choose bits of your drawing to pick up and move, or select bits of your drawing to duplicate.

The controls at the bottom (6) let you change the size of the shapes that you draw with, and change the colour by choosing from the palette. You can also use the colour picker to choose a colour from something you've already drawn.

The tools at the bottom right (7) will zoom out, reset the zoom to normal, or zoom in. At the top (8), you can use the buttons to undo a mistake you've made, or redo a change if you undo it and then change your mind.

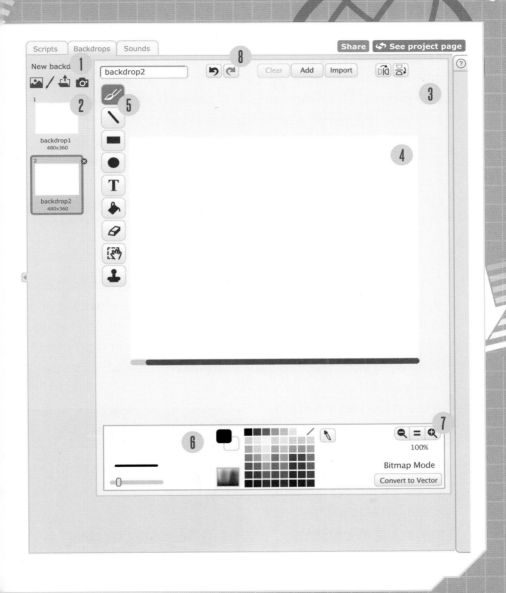

Scripts | Backdrops | Sounds

Share | See project page

New backdrop

1

2

backdrop1
480x360

2

backdrop2
480x360

8

backdrop2

Clear | Add | Import

3

5

T

4

6

100%

Bitmap Mode

Convert to Vector

7

1. Let's create a new Scratch project. So far we've been using a plain white backdrop, but let's start this time by making a different backdrop. In the bottom left of the screen is the sprites palette, which shows all of the different sprites you can use in your project. At the moment it just shows the cat. To the left of the cat sprite there's a picture of the stage and four options for changing the backdrop. You can choose one from the library, paint your own, upload one, or use your computer's camera to create one. We're going to paint our own, so click on the second option along (the one that looks like a paintbrush). We now have a blank white backdrop to edit and we're going to turn it into a racetrack to drive around.

2. First of all, let's fill the background with a green colour for the grass. Then use the paintbrush to draw the track. Move the line to the thickest setting so the track is nice and wide, and set it to a black colour so it looks like a road. Draw the track so it joins up, in a big loop. The new backdrop you've drawn should now be shown behind the cat in the stage window. If it's not, make sure the new backdrop is the one that's selected in the backdrops list on the left. If you want, you could also set the brush to thin and use white to draw the white lines down the centre of the track.

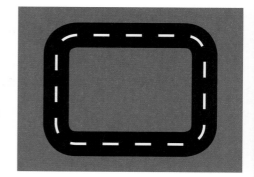

3. Next, we need to draw a racing car. The car is going to move around, which means it's a sprite and not a backdrop. The options for making a new sprite are in the top right of the sprite list, which is in the bottom left of the screen (where it says "New sprite"). Like the options for a new backdrop, you can choose a sprite from the library, paint your own, upload a picture, or take a photo with a camera. We're going to paint our own, so click on the picture of the brush.

4. The new sprite starts totally blank. We're going to draw our racing car in the middle, facing to the right side. A smaller car will be easier for you to race with. Start by drawing a red, filled rectangle, then draw four smaller grey rectangles along the sides to look like wheels. Then draw a small blue rectangle on one end of the car for the windscreen, so we know which end is the front. The final step is to use the "Set costume centre" button in the very top right of the sprite drawing window to set the centre of the sprite. Click on the button, then click in the middle of the car you've drawn.

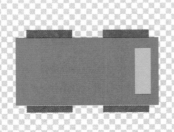

"Set costume centre" button

5. With our car now drawn, it should have appeared on the stage window. But the cat's still there! To delete the cat sprite, right-click on the sprite in the sprite list and then click on delete. It should immediately disappear from the stage. We also want our car to start on the track, so drag it on top of the track you've drawn in the stage window.

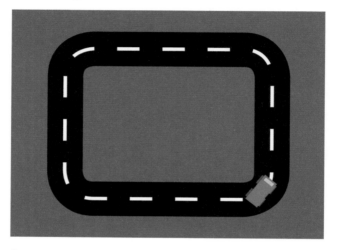

6. We've drawn a car and we've drawn a track, but the car isn't moving yet! We need to write some code for that. At the top of the right-hand side of the window, you can see three options: Scripts, Costumes and Sounds. If you've just drawn your car, costumes will be the selected option. Instead, choose Scripts. This should bring up the script area that we've used before.

7. Our car is going to have three inputs. When we press the right arrow key it should turn to the right, when we press the left arrow key it should turn to the left, and when we press the space bar it should start moving. The first two are quite similar – use the

"when space key pressed" Event block, but change the dropdown option to 'left arrow'. Then make another copy of it, but this time choose the 'right arrow' option. You can make a second copy by either dragging another "when space key pressed" block from the Event palette, or by right-clicking on the block you already have and choosing the 'duplicate' option from the menu. Next, underneath the left arrow key block, put the "Turn anticlockwise by 15 degrees" Motion block and under the right arrow key block, put the "Turn clockwise by 15 degrees" Motion block.

8. Try pressing the left and right arrow keys now, and you should see your sprite turning to the left and right!

9. Now to make the car move, take another "when space key pressed" Event block. We want the car to keep moving without stopping. That means it should keep doing the same thing forever on a loop. So we need to drop one of the "forever" Control blocks underneath the "when space key pressed" Event block. And the thing we want it to do forever is to move 5 steps, so take the "move 10 steps" Motion block, and change the 10 to a 5.

10. Okay, it's time to take your car for a test drive! (Tip: if you press the blue large-screen button to the top-left of the stage, it will fill up more of the screen.) When you're ready, press the space bar to start the car moving, and press the left and right arrows to steer it round the track. How many laps can you do without going off the edge of the track?

If the car goes off the side of the stage, it can be quite difficult to steer it back onto the track. If that happens, you can just press the red stop button above the stage, then press escape to exit full-screen mode. You can then click and drag the car back into the middle of the stage area.

Take it further...

1. Make your track more realistic by drawing white lines down the middle of the roads, or drawing trees around the edges. You could also make your car more realistic, too. Here's a suggestion – can you work out how to make one like this?

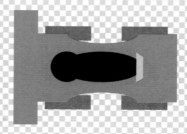

2. Make your track more difficult to drive around! Why not try drawing your track as a big figure of eight, instead of a circle?

3. Create faster or slower cars. Make a variable called "speed", which is going to say how fast the car should move. When the up arrow key is pressed, change the speed variable by 1 to make the car go faster. When the down arrow key is pressed, change the speed variable by -1 to make the car slower. The last step is to make the distance moved by the car inside the forever loop to be equal to the speed variable, instead of being fixed at 5. Now you should be able to drive the car and change its speed! What's the fastest speed you can do a full loop of the track on? Try pressing the down arrow key until the car is going in reverse. What's the fastest reverse speed you can do a loop of the track on?

CHAPTER 5: LOGIC
Asking questions and making choices

Have you ever thought about how you make decisions? You actually make decisions all the time without even thinking about it. When you're getting dressed in the morning on a school day, you probably put on your school uniform. But when you're getting dressed in the morning on a weekend, you probably put on normal clothes. When you do that, you're making a decision between two options based on the day of the week. The same decision could be written as "**if** it's a school day **then** wear school uniform **or if** it's a weekend **then** wear normal clothes."

This type of decision-making is called **logic**, and it's used a lot in all kinds of coding. For example, in a game there might be logic that says **if** the number of lives left is 0 **then** game over, **otherwise** carry on. Or a program for playing music might have logic that says **if** the playlist has more songs **then** play the next song **otherwise** stop playing music.

The test you use to make a decision is called a **condition**. All conditions can either be **true** or **false**. For example, the condition "the numbers of lives left is 0" is false when you have three lives left, and true when you have 0 lives left. Conditions let us write different lines of code to be run in different situations. You can write your code once to respond to every situation, without having to change it manually for every new event.

Using conditions in coding is sometimes called **Boolean Logic**, after the British mathematician George Boole who developed the mathematics of logic.

In Python

Python has six types of condition, shown in the table below. Be careful with the equals condition; it uses two equals signs not one. Python strings which have different numbers of spaces, or different capital letters are not equal: so "cat" is not equal to "Cat" or "CAT". Try out some of the examples shown below:

Name	Examples to try
Equals `==`	`3==3` is true, `"Anna"=="anna"` is false
Not equal `!=`	`"Anna"!="Bob"` is true, `3!=3` is false
Less than `<`	`3 < 4` is true, `4 < 3` is false
Greater than `>`	`5 > 3` is true, `3 > 5` is false
Less than or equal to `<=`	`3 <= 3` is true, `4 <= 3` is false
Greater than or equal to `>=`	`4 >= 4` is true, `3 >= 6` is false

To use conditions to make decisions, we'll need to use **if**. Try running the following code – make sure you type the **:** and type four extra spaces at the start of the second line, just like with loops. You'll need to leave the third line blank, so just press Enter again.

```
>>> if 3 < 4:
...     print("3 is less than 4")
...
3 is less than 4
```

Python checks to see whether 3 is less than 4, which is true. Because the condition was true, it then runs the indented line and writes out "3 is less than 4".

Now try this code:

```
>>> if 4 < 3:
...     print ("4 is less than 3")
...
```

This time, Python checks to see whether 4 is less than 3, which is false. Because the condition is false, Python doesn't run the indented line, so nothing gets written out.

The colon (:) after the condition, followed by a line that starts with four spaces, probably looks familiar – it's very similar to the code for a loop. And just like in a loop, you can have more than one indented line of code. In a loop, all the indented lines of code will be run again each time the loop is run, but inside the **if** condition, all the lines of code will only be run if the condition is true.

Just like with a loop, Python waits for you to type one blank line before running the code.

Conditions are most useful when we use them with variables so our programs can make decisions while they're running. Try running this code for checking a password. Type in **monkeys** when you're asked for the password. Make sure you remember to put indents at the start of both lines that print something, but not before the if or else. And remember the : after if and else!

```
>>> guess = input("What is the password? ")
>>> if guess == "parrots":
...     print("Correct password!")
... else:
...     print("Incorrect password.")
...
```

You should see Python say "Incorrect password". Now type in the code again, but this time type in **parrots** when you're asked for the password. This time, Python should say "Correct password!" Make sure that you don't accidentally type it with a capital letter, or any spaces.

This code works by using a special form of if which lets us say what code should be run if the condition is true, but also lets us write code to be run if the condition is false. We do that with the else keyword. else is written without extra spaces at the start, and is followed by a colon (:), then one or more lines of code to be run when the condition is false.

Just like with loops and if conditions, all the lines of code that should be run when the condition is false start on the line after the colon (:) and are indented by four spaces.

You can also put **if** and **else** conditions inside your loops. When you do that, you'll need to indent some of your code twice (so that it's indented by eight spaces instead of the usual four). Let's try that by writing some code that loops through the numbers from 0 to 10, but only prints them out if they're bigger than 5. Type in this code:

```
>>> for number in range(11):
...     if number > 5:
...         print(number)
...
```

and you should see

```
6
7
8
9
10
```

The first line of code is a loop that counts up to 10 in a variable called number. The second line is indented once (by four spaces), and checks to see if number is bigger than 5. The third line is indented twice (by eight spaces), so it's inside the loop and inside the **if** condition. If the number is bigger than 5, it'll be printed out on the terminal. Otherwise, the loop will just carry on.

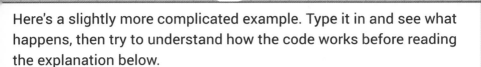

Here's a slightly more complicated example. Type it in and see what happens, then try to understand how the code works before reading the explanation below.

```
>>> for number in range(4):
...     print("Trying " + str(number))
...     if number < 2:
...         print("Smaller than 2")
...     else:
...         print("Not smaller than 2")
...     print("Finished with " + str(number))
...
Trying 0
Smaller than 2
Finished with 0
Trying 1
Smaller than 2
Finished with 1
Trying 2
Not smaller than 2
Finished with 2
Trying 3
Not smaller than 2
Finished with 3
```

We can get Python to do a lot of work with seven lines of code! The first line is a loop that will count from 0 to 3, as you've seen already. All of the other lines are indented by at least four spaces, so they are inside the loop, and will be run every time through the loop, as you learned in chapter 3.

The second line prints "Trying " and then the number. Remember, we have to convert the number to a string so that Python can print it, as you learned in chapter 1.

The third line checks whether the number is less than 2. If it is, the fourth line will be run. You can tell, because the fourth line is indented twice, by 8 spaces, and it will print "Smaller than 2".

The fifth line is only indented once, so it's inside the loop but not the **if** condition. If the number is not less than 2, the **else** condition code will be run instead. That's the sixth line of code, which will print "Not smaller than 2". The sixth line is indented by four more spaces than the fifth line, which tells you that it's inside the **else** condition.

The last line is only indented once — it's inside the loop but not the **if** or **else** conditions — so it will be run each time through the loop. After everything else that's being looped has been completed, it will say "Finished with " and then the number, before Python continues with the next number in the loop.

Python Puzzle Part 5

The three friends gathered around the screen to read the final clue.

The passcode is the answer to this riddle:
A farmer owns a number of cows and chickens on his
farm. He has less than 100 of each, but he has 22
more chickens than cows. Each chicken has 2 legs,
and each cow has 4 legs, and in total all of his
animals together have 296 legs. How many cows does
he have?

"Oh no, I'm rubbish at riddles," moaned Charlie. "How are we supposed to work that out?" Finn was thinking so hard he looked as though he might hurt himself. "I just don't see how we can use Python to help us here," he said finally.

Mia looked carefully at the clue. "I think we need to use an if condition to get the answer. Listen: we know that the number of cows is no more than 100, so we just need to loop through the number of cows up to 100. For each number, we calculate the number of chickens, the number of cow's legs, the number of chicken's legs and the total number of legs. If the total number of legs comes to 296, then print the number of cows. That should do it!"

It sounds like Mia's cracked it! Can you work out the passcode before she does? You'll need to use lots of the things you've learnt already, including loops, variables and conditions. You'll find the answer on page 134.

PASSCODE: _____

Hint:

```
>>> for cows in range (_____):
...      chickens = _____ + 22
...      cows_legs = _____ *
...      chickens_legs = _____ *
...      total_legs = _____ +
...      if _____ == 296:
...           print(_____)
```

"Nice one, Mia!" said Finn, with a grin. "Let's give it a go". As Finn typed the passcode into the computer, the door swung open and Aisha tumbled out onto the floor.

"We did it!" shouted Charlie, helping her up. "Took you guys long enough!" Aisha joked. But she looked seriously relieved to be free. "Let's get out of here."

The four of them turned and ran as fast as they could back the way they'd come. As they passed through each room, the doors slammed shut behind them. They sprinted back past the giant robot, through the room with 100 doors, round the trapdoor in the entrance hall and finally out of the huge front door. They didn't stop until they reached the woods and collapsed onto the ground, exhausted.

"That place was crazy!" said Aisha. "How on earth did you get through all those locked doors?"

Charlie sat up. "Well, it was lucky I was here really."

In Scratch

You've already seen that there are similarities between coding loops and conditions in Python. They're similar in Scratch too, because both types of blocks are in the Control palette.

Look in Scratch's Control palette now, and you should see two blocks for "if <> then", and "if <> then else". Just like the "repeat 10" block you've already used, you can drag other blocks inside these blocks. The "if <> then" block will only run the blocks inside it if the condition is true, and the "if <> then else" block will run all the blocks between the "if" line and the "else" line if the condition is true, and run all the blocks after the "else" line if the condition is false. That's just the same as "if" and "else" in Python.

To find conditions in Scratch (remember, conditions are the tests programs do to decide what code to run), look in the Sensing and Operators palettes. You can tell which blocks are conditions because they have pointed corners on the left and right sides.

In the Sensing palette, there are conditions for checking what the sprite, or some of the colours on it, are touching, and whether a key is being pressed on the keyboard or the mouse is being clicked.

It's easy to confuse the "key space pressed?" Sensing block with the "when space key pressed" Event block. The same goes for confusing the "mouse down?" Sensing block with the "when this sprite clicked" Event block, but they're actually used in different ways. The Sensing blocks let you check whether a key is being pressed, or the mouse is being clicked, and then decide what code to run. The Event blocks will be run whenever someone running your code clicks the mouse or presses a key. You could think of it like this: the Sensing blocks are like when you wake up naturally and then decide whether you need to get out of bed or not, and the Event blocks are like when your alarm goes off (or someone shouts at you!) to tell you that you need to get out of bed.

In the Operators palette, there are three conditions that should look familiar. Just like Python, Scratch has a "O>O" block and a "O<O" block for checking if one number is greater than or less than another, and a "O=O" block for checking if two things are equal (which only

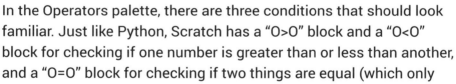

uses one equals sign, whereas Python uses two). Scratch doesn't have a way of checking for things being greater than or equal, or less than or equal, like Python does.

Let's try using these to create a password-checking program in Scratch. This will be similar to what we did in Python and, at the end, we'll be able to compare the two programs. The person using our program is going to type in a password. If it's right, we'll say "That's the right password!", and if it's wrong, we'll say "No, that isn't the password."

1. First of all, create a variable called "password guess". We're going to use that to store whatever is typed as the guess for the password.

2. Now we need to ask the user to tell us what they think the password is. Let's use the "ask What's your name? and wait" block from the Sensing palette, but change it to say "What's the password?" Now we want Scratch to take what they typed and put it into our variable "password guess". To do that, use the "set password guess to 0" block from the Data palette, and change the "0" to the "answer" block from the Sensing palette.

ask What's the password? and wait
set password guess ▾ to answer

3. Next, we need to check whether the password guess matches the actual password. If the password guess is equal to the password, we want Scratch to run one thing, and if the guess isn't equal to the password, we want Scratch to run something different. Take an "if <> then else" block from the Control palette and drag it into your script. In the "<>" area, drag the "0=0" block from the Operators palette. In one of the gaps in that block, type the word "parrots" (which will be the real password). In the other gap, drag the block for our "password guess" variable from the Data palette.

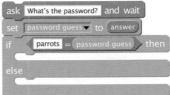

4. Any blocks we put inside the top half of the "if <> then else" block will be run by Scratch if the password guess is equal to

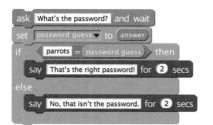

the actual password (which we decided is "parrots"). Drag the "say Hello! for 2 secs" block from Looks into the top half of the "if <> then else" block, and change it to "say That's the right password! for 2 secs". Do the same for the bottom half of the "if <> then else" block, but change it to "say No, that isn't the password. for 2 secs".

5. Now click the blocks to try out the program. When you're asked for the password, try typing "pirates" (or anything you like that isn't the word "parrots"). The cat should tell you that that is the wrong password. Try running it again, but this time type in "parrots". This time, Scratch should tell you that the password is right. You could use this to annoy your brothers, sisters, friends and parents by getting them to try and guess your password! (Tip: open the stage in full-screen mode first so they can't see the code.)

Look back at our password-checker in Python (see page 95). Even though Python and Scratch can look very different, our password-checker program actually looks very similar in both languages. They both ask the user to type in the password, and then store that in a variable. They use an "if" with a condition to check whether the password is right. If it is, they say so. If it isn't, they use an "else" to say something different. Even though Scratch uses colourful blocks you can move around, and is designed for learning to code, and Python uses text and is used for millions of things by professional coders, the way you code with them can be very similar.

Scratch Project 5

We're going to code another game! The game we're going to make is a bit like air hockey, and it's very similar to one of the earliest video games, called Pong. Pong is a computer game based on tennis, and it was very popular in the 1970s.

Pong is a game for two players (though you can also play it by yourself). There are two rectangles, one on each side of the screen, which are the 'tennis racquets' for each player. There's also a ball which bounces around the screen. Both players are trying to hit the ball with their racquets. If the ball goes past your opponent, you get one point.

1. Okay, let's start by putting the background in place. The original Pong game used a black background with a white ball and white racquets, so we're going to do the same. In the backdrop list in the bottom left of the screen, click on the plain white rectangle

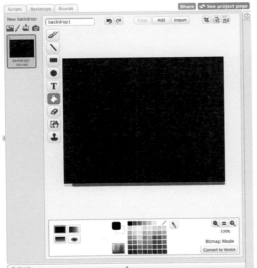

that represents the default backdrop, then click on the "Backdrops" tab at the top of the page. Now select the black colour from the palette at the bottom of the screen, and the "Fill with color" icon from the menu on the left of the backdrop. Click anywhere on the backdrop to turn it from white to black – you should see it change colour in the stage area too.

2. Next, let's draw a white line down the middle of the backdrop to show where the net would be on a real tennis court. Click on the "Line" icon from the menu on the left, then move the slider (which is on the left side of the palette) all the way to the left to draw very thin lines. Choose the white colour from the palette and then draw a straight line down the middle of the backdrop by dragging. You should see the line appear on the backdrop in the stage area too.

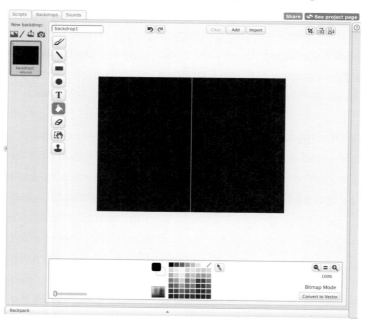

Here's a hint! To draw a really straight line, click and hold to start drawing the line, then hold the Shift button (⇧) while you draw the rest of the line. Only let go of Shift once you've let go of the mouse button to draw the line.

3. Before we go any further, delete the cat sprite by right-clicking on it and choosing "delete" from the menu. We won't need it for this game.

4. Now let's draw the racquets. To start drawing the first racquet, click on the "Paint new sprite" button just above the sprite list. I'm going to draw them as simple rectangles, but you can make them more exciting if you want. Choose the "Rectangle" tool, and a blue colour from the palette. To the left of the palette, you'll see an option to choose a filled-in rectangle, instead of the outline of a rectangle. Choose the filled-in option and then draw a narrow, vertical rectangle. Click anywhere on the stage to make it appear (you have to click away from the rectangle before it will appear on the stage). The taller the rectangle you draw, the easier the game will be.

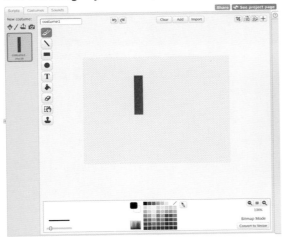

5. Now we need to make a second racquet. We could just draw another racquet for the other player, but a faster way is to duplicate the one we already have (which will also make sure they're exactly the same size). To do that, right click on the first racquet in the sprite list or on the stage, and choose duplicate. Move the first racquet you drew over to the left side of the stage, by dragging it. Drag the copy over to the right-hand side of the stage.

x: -240 y: 180

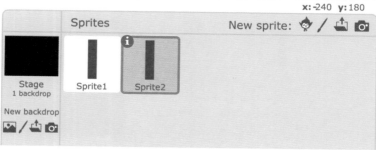

6. The last sprite we'll need is our ball. We could draw our own (and you can if you want to), but I'm going to choose an existing one from Scratch. Click on "Choose sprite from library" above the sprite list, go to "Things" and double-click on the tennis ball.

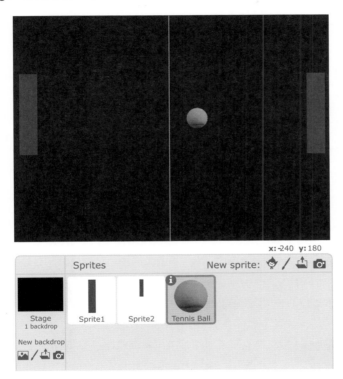

x: -240 y: 180

7. Now we've got all of our sprites in place, we need to start telling Scratch what to do with them. We're going to have a few different scripts in our game, and we want them all to happen at the same time. To make that happen, we're going to start all of our scripts with the "when green flag clicked" event.

8. Let's start with the left racquet. We need to start by writing a script to make it move. One player is going to be using "Q" on the keyboard to make it go up, and "A" on the keyboard to make it go down. To make that happen, we need the game to be constantly checking whether one of those keys is being pressed, and then to move the racquet in the correct direction. Choose the left racquet (which should be called "Sprite 1") from the sprites list, then click on the

"Scripts" tab. Start the script with the "when green flag clicked" block from the Events palette, and put a "forever" loop from the Control palette underneath it. We've used the forever loop before to keep running the same code over and over again.

9. Inside the loop, we need to check whether the "Q" key is being pressed. And if it is, we want the racquet to move up. To do this, take the "if <> then" block from the Control palette, and put it inside the "forever" block. The condition we need is the "key space pressed?"

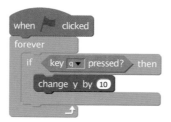

block from the Sensing palette, so drag that into the "<>" space of the "if <> then" block. Change it to say "key q pressed?" Then take the "change y by 10" block from the Motion palette, and drag it inside the "if" block, so that it will only be run when the "Q" key is pressed.

10. Now we need to do the same thing to move the racquet down when the "A" key is pressed. Take another "if <> then" block and drag it inside the "forever" loop, underneath the bottom of the "if key q pressed?" block. It's very important to make sure this goes in the right place – it must not be inside the "if" block we already have, but it must be inside the "forever" block.

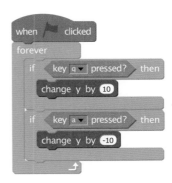

Take another "key space pressed?" block into the second "if" block and change it to say "key a pressed?". Inside that "if", drag another "change y by 10" block, but change it to say "-10".

11. Let's check the script we've written so far works. Click on the green flag, and try pressing the "Q" and "A" keys. You should see the left racquet move up when you press "Q" and down when you press "A". Cool, huh?! Press the red stop button to stop the scripts running.

12. Now we need to write scripts for the other racquet. This racquet will be used by the other player, and they will move it up and down by pressing the "P" and "L" keys on the keyboard. First, click on the other racquet in the sprites list (which should be called "Sprite 2"). Then follow the instructions for the other racquet, but use the "P" key instead of the "Q" key, and the "L" key instead of the "A" key.

13. Let's check that everything is working so far. Click on the green flag, then try pressing the "Q" and "A" buttons to move the left racquet up and down, and the "P" and "L" buttons to move the right racquet up and down. Your game is starting to take shape!

14. Now we need to write a script for moving the ball, so click on the Tennis Ball sprite. Again, we're going to begin this script with

a "when green flag clicked" event and a "forever" loop. The most important thing for the ball to do is move around, so let's start with that. Drag a "move 10 steps" block from the Motion palette and drop it inside the "forever" loop.

15. If you click on this script to run it, you'll see the ball move straight to one side and stay there. We need to make it bounce when

it gets to the edge. To do that, take the "if on edge, bounce" block from the Motion palette, and drag it into the "forever" block underneath the "move 10 steps" block. Run the script again and the ball should start bouncing from side to side.

16. At the moment, the ball is travelling right through the racquets, not bouncing off them! Let's fix that. First, we need to use an "if <> then" block, inside the "forever" block, before the "move 10 steps". Make sure it goes before the "move 10 steps" and "if on edge, bounce" blocks, not around them.

17. The ball should bounce when it touches the left racquet or the right racquet. We can check for those conditions with the "<> or <>" block from the Operators palette, so drag that into the "<>" of the "if" block. We want the ball to bounce when it hits either of the racquets, so drag two of the "touching ?" blocks from the Sensing palette into each side of the "<> or <>" block. Each sprite in Scratch has a name, which you can see underneath the sprite in the sprite list. Change the "touching ?" blocks so that they each say the name of one of the racquet sprites (which will be "Sprite 1" and "Sprite 2" if you've been following along closely).

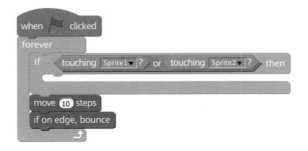

18. Now we need to write the code to make the ball bounce. To do that, drag a "point in direction 90" block from the Motion palette, and drop it inside the "if" we just created. Take a "O - O" block from the Operators block, and put that inside the "point in direction" block, replacing the 90. Drag the "direction" block from the Motion palette into the right-hand side of the "O - O". In the left-hand side, drag a "pick random from 1 to 10" block from the Operators palette, but change it to say "pick random from 340 to 380". If you find it hard to put the "pick random from 1 to 10" block" into the right part of the "O - O" operator, try dragging it so the left-hand side of the "pick random from 1 to 10" block is directly over one of the "O" gaps.

You should see a white outline around the "O" – that tells you that the block will go into the gap when you let go of the mouse.

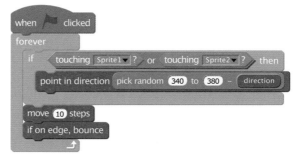

19. Let's also tell Scratch to make a sound when the ball bounces off a racquet. From the Sound palette, drag a "play sound pop" block, and drag it underneath the "point in direction" block we just used, inside the "if" block.

```
when 🏴 clicked
forever
    if   touching Sprite1 ? or touching Sprite2 ? then
        point in direction pick random 340 to 380 - direction
        play sound pop ▼

    move 10 steps
    if on edge, bounce
```

20. With this last bit of code, when the ball comes into contact with either of the racquets, it will bounce in a slightly random direction and make a small sound. It's time to press the green flag and try the game you've created! Remember you can move the left racquet with "Q" and "A", and the right racquet with "P" and "L". Can you stop the ball from hitting the left or right sides of the stage area? Why not find someone to play Pong with? Each time the ball hits the wall behind your opponent's racquet, you get a point. Make the stage full-screen for the best effect. First player to 5 points wins!

Getting faster

1. At the moment, the ball moves at the same speed all the time, but it might be more fun if the ball got faster and faster as the game went on. Make sure you still have the Tennis Ball sprite selected, and then make a variable called "speed" (remember: you can make variables in the Data palette). If you're asked whether to make the variable "for this sprite only", leave the checkbox unticked.

2. As soon as you do that, Scratch will put a little box in the stage area to show the value of the speed variable. In the Data palette, there's a checkbox next to the speed variable – untick the checkbox to make that disappear.

3. Every time a game is started, we should reset the speed, otherwise the ball will start at the same speed it had in the last game (or it will be 0 and the ball won't move at all). We're going to do this in a separate script from the one we already have with a "forever" loop in. So drag a new "when green flag clicked" block from the Events palette, into the scripts area, somewhere near the script we already have. Underneath it, drag the "set speed to 0" block, but change it to say "set speed to 6".

4. We should also make sure the ball is reset to the middle of the stage, facing one of the racquets, every time the green flag is clicked. That way our game will be properly reset. Take a "go to x: y:" block from the Motion palette and drag it under the "set speed to 6" block, then change it to "go to x:0 y:0". (When you see the block in the Motion palette, it will show the current position of the sprite, for example "go to x:88 y:18" – don't let that put you off!)

5. Take a "point in direction 90" block from the Motion palette too, and drag that underneath the "go to x:0 y:0" block. That will move the ball back to the middle and make it point to the right every time we click the green flag.

6. We want to increase the speed every time the ball hits one of the racquets. We already have some code that runs when a ball hits a racquet: it's the code that makes the ball bounce and plays a sound. From the Data palette, drag a "change speed by 1" block and drop it underneath the "play sound pop" block, but still inside the "if" block.

7. To make the ball actually move faster, we can't just change the value of the "speed" variable, we have to use it somewhere as well.

Instead of moving 10 steps every time through the loop, the ball should move as far as the speed variable says. So open the Data palette, and drag the "speed" variable into the "move 10 steps" block we already have, so that it says "move speed steps".

```
when 🏳 clicked
forever
    if  touching Sprite1 ▾ ?  or  touching Sprite2 ▾ ?  then
        point in direction  pick random 340 to 380 – direction
        play sound pop ▾
        change speed ▾ by 1
    move speed steps
    if on edge, bounce
```

Now the ball will start moving more slowly, but will get faster and faster every time it's hit. Try it with a friend! How many consecutive hits of the ball can you do without the ball going past a racquet?

Keeping score

The final thing we need to do is to keep score. Remember, the right-hand player wins a point if the ball goes behind the left-hand racquet and the left-hand player wins a point if the ball goes behind the right-hand racquet.

1. The first thing we should do is create variables to keep track of each player's score. Make sure you've selected the sprite of the ball in the sprites list, then go to the Data palette and create a variable called "left player score" and another called "right player score".

You can call these variables whatever you want, like your own name and your friend's name, for example. You can also rename them at any time to match the names of the players by finding the variable in the Data palette, right-clicking on it, then choosing "rename variable". But I'm going to call them "left player score" and "right player score" for now.

2. Both variables will appear in the stage area. Drag them around so that the left player's score is in the top-left of the stage, and the right player's score is in the top-right of the stage. Double-click on both of the scores, so that the name of the variable disappears and only the value is shown.

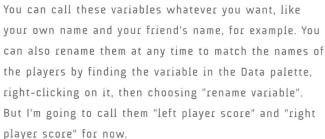

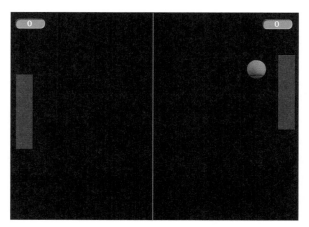

3. Now we need to work out when each player has scored a point, and change the scores appropriately. To do that, we're going to use Scratch to detect when the ball hits a certain colour. Click on the black backdrop in the stage area, then click on the Backdrops tab. Along the left edge, draw a very thin, red rectangle. Make sure it is the full height of the backdrop, but very thin. Choose a red colour from the palette, then choose the rectangle tool, and select the solid rectangle option (just like when you drew the racquets). Now do exactly the same thing on the right edge, but with a very thin green rectangle.

4. Choose the tennis ball sprite again from the sprites list, and click on the Scripts tab. We're now going to write some code that is only run when the ball touches the red rectangle behind the left racquet. Take an "if <> then" block from the Control palette, and drag it underneath the big "if touching Sprite1? or touching Sprite2? then" block, above the "move speed steps". Be careful not to put it around the "move speed steps" block or the "if on edge, bounce" block. If that happens, drag out the blocks from inside the new "if <> then" block and drop them underneath it (but still inside the "forever" block).

```
when [flag] clicked
forever
    if < touching Sprite1 ? or touching Sprite2 ? > then
        point in direction pick random 340 to 380 - direction
        play sound pop
        change speed by 1
    if <> then

    move speed steps
    if on edge, bounce
```

5. We want Scratch to check whether the ball is touching the red colour that only appears at the far left of the stage. So, take a "touching color?" block and drag it inside the condition of the new "if <> then" block. Now click on the coloured square in the "touching color?" block, and then click on the red rectangle at the far left of the stage. The square should change to be red. If you made your rectangle very thin, you'll have to be very careful

```
when [flag] clicked
forever
    if  < touching [Sprite1 ▼] ? > or < touching [Sprite2 ▼] ? > then
        point in direction ( pick random (340) to (380) ) – ( direction )
        play sound [pop ▼]
        change [speed ▼] by (1)

    if  < touching color [ ] ? > then

    move (speed) steps
    if on edge, bounce
```

to click on it – you can check by seeing what colour the square becomes. You'll also see the square turn red before you click if your mouse is in the right position.

6. Now we need to think about what should happen when the ball touches that red left edge. The player on the right should get one extra point, and we should also reset the game ready for the next point. To give the player one extra point, take a "change speed by

```
when [flag] clicked
forever
    if  < touching [Sprite1 ▼] ? > or < touching [Sprite2 ▼] ? > then
        point in direction ( pick random (340) to (380) ) – ( direction )
        play sound [pop ▼]
        change [speed ▼] by (1)

    if  < touching color [ ] ? > then
        change [right player score ▼] by (1)
        go to x: (0) y: (0)
        set [speed ▼] to (6)

    move (speed) steps
    if on edge, bounce
```

1" block from the Data palette, and drag it inside the "if" block, then change it to say "change right player score by 1". To get the game ready for the next point, drag a "go to x: y:" block from the Motion palette into the "if" block as well, and change it to say "go to x: 0 y: 0". That will move the ball back to the centre, but we also need to reset the speed. Drag a "set speed to 0" block from the Data palette into the "if" block, and change it to say "set speed to 6".

7. We now need to do almost exactly the same thing for the other side. When the ball touches the thin green rectangle, we should "change left player score by 1", and then reset the ball's position and speed ready for the next point in the same way. Try clicking the green flag, and play a few points of Pong! If the ball is already moving, you might need to first press the red stop button above the stage.

```
when     clicked
forever
    if     touching Sprite1 ▾ ?   or   touching Sprite2 ▾ ?   then
        point in direction  pick random  340  to  380  –  direction
        play sound  pop ▾
        change  speed ▾  by  1

    if     touching color    ? then
        change  right player score ▾  by  1
        go to x: 0  y: 0
        set  speed ▾  to  6

    if     touching color    ? then
        change  left player score ▾  by  1
        go to x: 0  y: 0
        set  speed ▾  to  6

    move  speed  steps
    if on edge, bounce
```

Now click the green flag again, to start a new game. Oops, we forgot to reset the scores! When the green flag is clicked, the scores should go back to 0.

8. To do that, let's add "set right player score to 0" and "set left player score to 0" blocks from the Data palette, and put them underneath our smaller script, beneath the "point in direction 90" block.

Now try clicking the green flag again, and the scores should reset. Ask a friend or a family member to play against you! (Tip: make the stage full screen before playing.)

when ⚑ clicked
forever
  if < touching Sprite1 ? or touching Sprite2 ? > then
    point in direction (pick random 340 to 380 – direction)
    play sound pop
    change speed by 1
  if < touching color ? > then
    change right player score by 1
    go to x: 0 y: 0
    set speed to 6
  if < touching color ? > then
    change left player score by 1
    go to x: 0 y: 0
    set speed to 6
  move speed steps
  if on edge, bounce

when ⚑ clicked
set speed to 6
go to x: 0 y: 0
point in direction 90▾
set right player score to 0
set left player score to 0

Take it further...

- Draw a different background, or more colourful racquets! But make sure you don't use the red or green colours that are at the far left and right of the backdrop.
- Make the ball speak when one of the players wins a point. You can do that with the "say Hello! for 2 secs" from the Looks palette, but changed to say "Left player wins a point!" or "Right player wins a point!" You could even use your name and the name of your friend!
- Give the players a moment to catch their breath in between points. Use the "wait 1 secs" block from the Control palette to put a small pause at the very start of the game, and at the end of each point.

In this chapter, you learned all about how to make your programs decide whether or not code should be run. You learned about how to use conditions in Python and Scratch, and writing "if" and "else" code that uses them. These are very common in all kinds of coding, so understanding them is very important.

CONCLUSION

Congratulations! You're a coder!

If you've read and understood everything in this book, then you're well on the way to being an incredible coder.

In **chapter 1**, you learned about how you can use variables to store and reuse data in your programs, which is vital for keeping track of things that change in code (like the number of lives a player has left, or a character's position on the screen).

In **chapter 2**, you learned about using different types of data, like strings and integers, and how to convert between them. As you experiment more with coding, you'll find this is really useful for combining together input data with your variables to make output.

In **chapter 3**, you learned about using loops to run the same code lots of times. This can save you lots of time in coding, and lets you write code that can do the same thing again and again.

In **chapter 4**, you learned about different kinds of input you can use in your programs, and how to use it. Input will let you write code that can respond to users clicking things and typing things. It makes your code come alive!

In **chapter 5**, you learned how to write programs that make decisions and can choose what code to run depending on different conditions. Conditions let you write code that does different things for different users, depending on the input. They help you make your code intelligent.

The brilliant thing about coding is you can now invent and make your own games, programs and animations, then show your family and friends. Or just use it to help with your maths homework! Adapting code can be really fun too – you just need to start by finding some code that's similar to what you want to make, either by asking an adult to help you search online, or by taking code from this book. Then you can read the code through until you understand how it works. Then you can change the code to make your own project, and try it out. By exploring what other people have made, and playing with it, you can make your own unique creations.

In this book, you've learned the basic skills you need to become a great coder, but you're not a master yet! You can take your coding further by practising and challenging yourself with new things to make. Even the best coders are always learning new things, and experimenting with their code.

If you'd like to learn more about Scratch, you can see some cool example projects by going to the homepage at scratch.mit.edu and clicking on "See examples". You can also watch tutorials that explain how to do things in Scratch by clicking "Help" on the top bar of the Scratch home page, then clicking the link to the "Video tutorials".

Here are some ideas of things you can make with Scratch and Python:

1. Write a short story with three different characters who have a conversation, move around and change colour. Then animate your short story as a Scratch project.

2. Make a Scratch band! Draw several different characters on the screen, then add scripts to them so that they all make different sounds or musical notes when you click them. See what you can play with your band!

3. Make a Python number guessing game. Each time you type the following code into Python it will choose a random number between 1 and 100, then ask to you guess a number. What do you think will happen if your guess is too low, too high or spot on? Give it a go – can you guess the number within 20 guesses? Try it out on other people too. Do you think you could change it to create a different game?

```
>>> import random
>>> target = random.randint(1,100)
>>> for turn in range(20):
...     guess = int(input("Guess a number "))
...     if guess == target:
...         print("That's right!")
...     if guess < target:
...         print("Go higher")
...     if guess > target:
...         print("Go lower")
```

I hope this book is just the start of your journey in coding. Coding is one of the most fun and rewarding skills I've ever learned. It will be useful to you throughout your life – in school and afterwards – and it will let you make incredible, fun, unique projects and express yourself! So go and play with some code and have fun!

Answers

page 36 Python Puzzle Part 1
PASSCODE: 123456789
Your finished code should look like this:

```
>>> age = 31
>>> coordinates_of_manor = 128467
>>> number_of_pigeons = 2
>>> passcode = age * age * coordinates_of_manor +
number_of_pigeons
>>> print(passcode)
```

page 37
Answer 1:

```
>>> seconds_in_an_hour = 60*60
>>> seconds_in_a_day = seconds_in_an_hour * 24
>>> print(seconds_in_a_day)
86400
```

Answer 2:
part a)

```
>>> wives = 7
>>> sacks = wives * 7
>>> cats = sacks * 7
>>> kits = cats * 7
>>> print (kits)
2401
```

part b)

Including the "man with seven wives", there are

```
>>> 1 + wives + sacks + cats + kits
2801
```

in total being met in the poem. But the riddle asks how many were going to St. Ives – which is only one: the narrator of the poem!

page 45 Take it further...

1.

```
when  clicked
say Hello! for 2 secs
ask Tell me a number and wait
set number 1 ▼ to answer
ask Tell me another number and wait
set number 2 ▼ to answer
say If you multiply those together, you'll get... for 2 secs
say (number 1 * number 2) for 2 secs
```

2.

```
when  clicked
play sound meow ▼
say Hello! for 2 secs
play sound meow ▼
ask Tell me a number and wait
set number 1 ▼ to answer
play sound meow ▼
ask Tell me another number and wait
set number 2 ▼ to answer
play sound meow ▼
say If you multiply those together, you'll get... for 2 secs
play sound meow ▼
say (number 1 * number 2) for 2 secs
```

page 51 Python Puzzle Part 2
PASSWORD: 177toffees13

Mia realized the age multiplied by 3 and the favourite number needed to be converted into strings before they could be joined with the favourite sweets.

Your finished code should look like this:

```
>>> age = 59
>>> age_times_three = age * 3
>>> sweets = "toffees"
>>> favourite_number = 13
>>> password = str(age_times_three) + sweets +
str(favourite_number)
>>> print(password)
177toffees13
```

page 52

```
>>> print (str(number_1) + " multiplied by " +
str(number_2) + " is " + str(answer))
```

page 57 Take it further...

1.

```
when [flag] clicked
play sound [meow ▼]
say [Hello!] for (2) secs
play sound [meow ▼]
ask [What's your name?] and wait
set [name ▼] to (answer)
play sound [meow ▼]
say (join [Hello] (name)) for (2) secs
play sound [meow ▼]
ask [How are you feeling?] and wait
set [mood ▼] to (answer)
play sound [meow ▼]
say (join [I also feel] (mood)) for (2) secs
```

2.

```
when [flag] clicked
change size by (10)
say [Hello!] for (2) secs
change size by (10)
ask [What's your name?] and wait
set [name ▼] to (answer)
change size by (10)
say (join [Hello] (name)) for (2) secs
change size by (10)
ask [How are you feeling?] and wait
set [mood ▼] to (answer)
change size by (10)
say (join [I also feel] (mood)) for (2) secs
```

Or combine both:

```
when [flag] clicked
play sound [meow ▼]
change size by (3)
say [Hello!] for (2) secs
play sound [meow ▼]
change size by (10)
ask [What's your name?] and wait
set [name ▼] to (answer)
play sound [meow ▼]
change size by (10)
say (join [Hello] (name)) for (2) secs
play sound [meow ▼]
change size by (10)
ask [How are you feeling?] and wait
set [mood ▼] to (answer)
play sound [meow ▼]
change size by (10)
say (join [I also feel] (mood)) for (2) secs
```

page 65 Python Puzzle Part 3
Correct door: door 67

```
>>> for door in range (100):
...     print("door number")
...     print(door)
...     print("Answer is")
...     print(door * (door + 1))
```

In the output, you should see that door 67 leads to the right answer of 4556.

page 66 Changing Variables
1. Decrease number_of_lives by 1 (e.g. if a player lost a life in a game).
2. Turn answer from a number into a string (e.g. so that it's ready to be joined to another string, to be printed).
3. Multiply the number of points by 10 (e.g. if a player had picked up a bonus in a game).

page 67
1.
```
>>> for number in range (13):
...     answer = 7*number
...     print ("7 times " + str(number) + " is " +
str(answer))
```

Because we used range(13), Python should go up to 12 in the output. So the first line of your output should be:

```
7 times 0 is 0
```
and the last line should be:
```
7 times 12 is 84
```

2.
```
>>> total = 0
>>> for number in range (1000):
...      total = total + number
...      print(total)
```

You should see Python give you the answer 499500.

page 73 Take it further...
1.

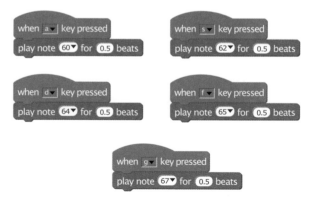

2.

pages 77–78

1.
```
>>> name = input("What name shall I reverse? ")
>>> backwards_name = name[::-1]
>>> print(backwards_name)
```

2.
```
>>> age_years = input("How old are you? ")
>>> months_since_birthday = input("How many months
since your last birthday? ")
>>> months_old = 12*int(age_years) + int(months_
since_birthday)
>>> print(months_old)
```

page 81 Python Puzzle Part 4
```
>>> for time in range(6):
...         robot_number = input("What did the robot
say? ")
...         number = int(robot_number)
...         answer = 9*number - 3
...         print(answer)
```

You will have entered the following six inputs: 399756, 482, 700813, 2078, 652001 and 1372. You should get the following six passcodes: 3597801, 4335, 6307314, 18699, 5868006 and 12345.

So the final passcode is 12345.

page 99 Python Puzzle Part 5

```
>>> for cows in range (101):
...     chickens = cows + 22
...     cows_legs = cows*4
...     chickens_legs = chickens*2
...     total_legs = cows_legs + chickens_legs
...     if total_legs == 296:
...         print(cows)
...
42
```

NOTES